Famous
Mineral Localities of
Canada

Famous Mineral Localities of Canada

by Joel D. Grice

National Museum of Natural Sciences

Published by Fitzhenry & Whiteside Limited

Published by Fitzhenry & Whiteside
195 Allstate Parkway
Markham, Ontario L3R 4T8

Written, designed, and typeset in Canada
Printed and bound by Wing King Tong (Hong Kong)

Editor: Glenys Popper
Designer: Gregory/Gregory Limited
Typesetter: Jay Tee Graphics Ltd.

Canadian Cataloguing in Publication Data

Grice, Joel
  Famous mineral localities of Canada

Co-published by the National Museum of Natural Sciences.
Issued also in French under title: Sites miniers
célèbres du Canada.
Bibliography: p.
ISBN 0-88902-898-2

1. Mines and mineral resources – Canada – History.
2. Mineralogy – Canada. I. National Museum of
Natural Sciences (Canada). II. Title.

QE376.G74 1989   553'.0971   C88-093836-6

Contents

5

Illustrations

Author's Preface

In Canada hundreds of "famous mineral localities" exist and my biased choice merely represents a selected variety of minerals, their uses and different geological environments. Since Canada is particularly rich in mineral and fuel resources, almost a third of the total value of her exports derives from these commodities. Canada has become the Western World's leading producer of nickel, zinc, asbestos and nepheline and the second largest producer of tantalum, silver, uranium, columbium, selenium, gypsum, molybdenum, potash and titanium. In this book I hope to encourage an interest in and promote an understanding of some of the basic concepts of mineralogy and geology, and instill an appreciation of the importance to everyone of these natural resources.

Joel D. Grice

Acknowledgments

The writing of this book involved many individuals and companies. I would like especially to thank Bob Gault for his assistance in the field and in the preparation of the Locality Mineral Lists, and Ruth Dinn who patiently prepared the many drafts of the manuscript.

The following, listed geographically, from west to east, provided information or field assistance: Cassiar Mining Ltd, Vancouver; Indian and Northern Affairs, Yukon Territorial Government; Cominco Ltd, Vancouver; Rose Gobiel, Grand Forks; Mr and Mrs Sid Baker, Kamloops; Mr and Mrs Sands, Rosedale; International Minerals & Chemical Corp. (Canada) Ltd, Esterhazy; Tantalum Mining Corp. of Canada Ltd, Bernic Lake; Mr Tom Stott, Wawa; The Algoma Steel Corp. Ltd, Sault Ste Marie; Falconbridge Ltd, Toronto; Inco Ltd, Toronto; Mr George Farr, Wilberforce; Mr Doug Robinson, Haileybury; Mr H. Meyn of Epitek International Inc., Ottawa; Carrière R. Poudrette Inc., Mont St-Hilaire; JM Asbestos Inc., Montreal; the Polar Continental Shelf Project and Mr Henry Webb, Nain. Photographs are individually credited. The author gratefully acknowledges this support.

Particularly important in the preparation of this book were: Bob Gait, Royal Ontario Museum, Toronto, for his critical review and suggestions; Jack Schekkerman, Ottawa, for the mineral photographs; and Jennifer Ball, Ottawa, for research and technical editing.

1
Geological Regions of Canada

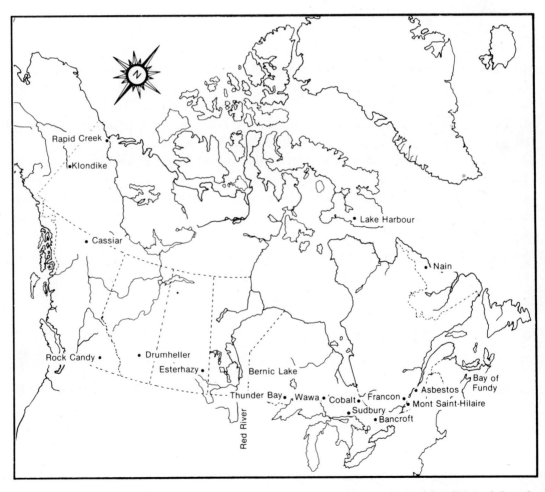

Famous mineral localities of Canada

Those fortunate people who have travelled part or all of the six thousand kilometres that comprise the breadth of Canada will have noted stunning differences in the surface features of the countryside. Four main physiographic regions divide the country: rough, spectacular mountain ranges of the Cordilleran rim the west side of the Continent; great expanses of flat prairie mark the Interior Platform; rugged country of hard, resistant rock cut by innumerable lakes and rivers comprises the core of the Continent — the Canadian Shield; and worn mountains and hills of the Appalachians extend along the eastern margins of Canada. These physiographic regions depend directly on the underlying geology. Each of the four geological regions has a distinct suite of rocks, differing from each other in age and provenance. Although the details of any region are complex, some general statements may help towards the understanding of the specific mineral localities described in subsequent chapters.

Canadian Shield
The Canadian, or Precambrian, Shield constitutes the stable core of the North American Continent. These ancient rocks vary in age from a billion to over three billion years, making them some of the oldest rocks in the world. They formed deep in the primaeval crust of planet Earth and lie exposed today after billions of years of erosion by rain, ice and wind. The original rocks underwent tortuous changes in temperature and pressure, producing a series of highly metamorphosed, coarsely crystalline rocks.

The Shield, named in allusion to its shape, constitutes approximately half of Canada's land surface and boasts one of the most productive mining areas in the world. Rich deposits of copper, nickel, iron, lead, zinc, gold, silver, cobalt, uranium, platinum, titanium and molybdenum support Canada's economy.

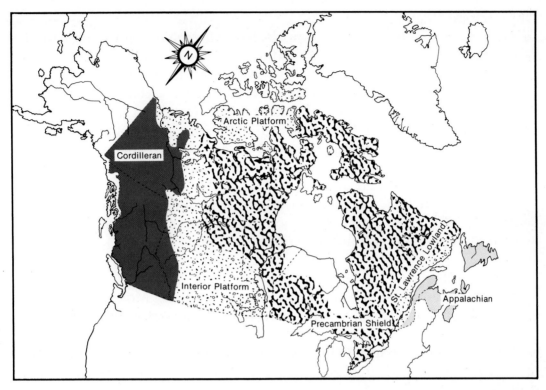

The major geological regions of Canada.

Platform Regions

The Platform, a series of flat-lying sedimentary rocks, overlies the Canadian Shield in a broad collar around its southern and western rim. This geological feature is evident in the St Lawrence Lowlands, the Interior Plains of the Midwest and the Arctic Lowlands to the north. The sediments, which derived from the Shield, Cordilleran or Appalachian regions and were deposited in seas that formerly covered the Shield, form a thin veneer on the Shield, excepting the western prairies where they attain thicknesses of several kilometres. The Interior Plains produce most of Canada's petroleum and natural gas as well as potash, salt, gypsum and limestone. During the ice age, soils ground from the Shield were deposited on the Platform. In the southern prairies and the St Lawrence valley, this fragile layer of sediments produced fertile agricultural land; unfortunately much of this is now covered by urban sprawl.

Appalachian Region

In North America, the old, worn Appalachian Mountains stretch three thousand kilometres; from Newfoundland to Alabama. They form the eastern coastline from Newfoundland to New York, but further south a flat plain of sedimentary rock separates them from the Atlantic Ocean. Formerly the Appalachian Region consisted of a submerged trough on the edge of the Shield. Over a period of hundreds of millions of years it was filled with sediments derived from the continent and ocean. Approximately four hundred million years ago these sediments uplifted to form a range of mountains, now largely eroded away.

The Appalachian Region, including the Atlantic provinces and southeastern Quebec, produces a good proportion of the world's asbestos as well as significant amounts of copper and zinc.

Cordilleran Region

Canada's newest mountains are part of the Cordilleran Mountain Region, which spans half the world — eighteen thousand kilometres from the Aleutian Islands to the tip of South America. This series of sedimentary and volcanic rocks heaved up approximately a hundred million years ago as a result of the collision of two huge continental plates. The theory of continental drift describes the flow of such crustal plates on the melted upper portions of the earth's interior. The interaction resulting from the collision of the American plate and the Pacific Ocean plates remains in evidence today in the activity of the volcanoes and earthquakes along the Pacific Ocean coastline. In Canada the Cordilleran Region displays itself in the spectacular Rocky Mountains and Coast Mountains of British Columbia.

Between the western and eastern mountain ranges the central plateau affords some opportunity for farming. With persistent geological surveying the Cordilleran has yielded important deposits of lead, zinc, silver, copper and gold.

The following chapters describe nineteen localities from the various geological regions of Canada. The number nineteen bears no significance in itself but the distribution gives evidence that some geological environments contain more mineral resources than others. The presentation of localities follows a west-to-east pattern and readers should gain a sense of the vast potential underlying Canada's geological regions.

2

Klondike Gold Rush

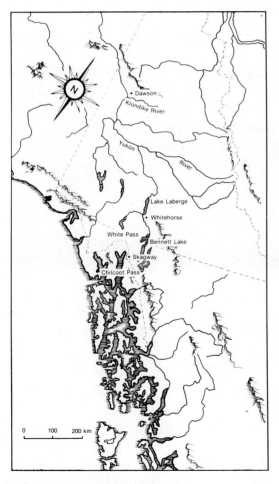

Klondike Gold Rush Area.

Gold Fever

Summer 1897, one year after the discovery of gold by Carmack on Bonanza Creek and Henderson on Gold Bottom Creek, the rush was on. Of the hundred thousand men and women who left their homes to seek their fortunes on the Yukon gold trails only forty thousand determined souls survived the formidable hardships and reached Dawson. About half of them actually prospected in the fields and of these a mere handful realized their dream of riches; but all of these characters, some more famous than others, played a role in the great Klondike gold rush.

Each and every "trail of '98" was perilous. The deceptive Skagway Trail across the White Pass brought many men to disaster. What began as a leisurely route through rolling hills turned into a nightmare of switchbacks and narrow corkscrew turns over several mountains and ridges. A single faulty step on the slippery slate cliffs of Devil's Hill

15

Some of the beauty along the gold rush route
near Whitehorse, Yukon. *Hans Blohm,*
Masterfile.

could plunge man or beast one hundred and fifty metres into the sheer valley below. Strewn with huge boulders, Porcupine Hill challenged the weary
to conquer its cumbersome, twisting path that led to Summit Hill's three-
hundred-metre climb: a slope strewn with shards of broken granite and
streams of slimy mud. Yet two more mountains still challenged the survivors.

Bonanza Creek, with Gold Hill to the right, at the height of the gold rush. Here in 1897 Carmack made his historic discovery that changed the Klondike forever. *MacBride Museum Collection/Yukon Archives.*

Bonanza Creek Basin at the confluence of the Klondike and Yukon rivers, showing the workings of dredge No. 3. *Public Archives Canada.*

For many Klondike miners equipment was
limited: a pick, a shovel and a sluice box.
Public Archives Canada.

Five thousand men and women attempted this seventy-kilometre passage
during the fall of 1897 but only a few reached Bennett Lake in time to navigate
the Yukon River to Dawson before freeze-up. The remainder had to camp
on the trail for the winter or turn back. During that fall three thousand pack
animals died of exhaustion and starvation on the Skagway. This incredible
cruelty and madness lived on as shameful memories in all witnesses.

There were few smiles on the streets of Dawson, where the harsh realities of life in the Klondike gold fields were readily exposed. *Public Archives Canada.*

Certainly Chilkoot Pass stands out in the history of the Klondike gold rush as a symbol of endurance. Over half of the fortune seekers took this trail, which involved a thousand-metre climb too steep to be negotiated by horses. Men became the pack animals, carrying loads of a hundred kilograms up the ice-carved steps with the perils of blizzards, high winds and fatal avalanches. As it was usual to have a tonne of gear, most men had to scale the Pass several times. Alternatively a man could pay two or three dollars a kilogram to professional packers.

For those making the expedition, high demands were made upon purse, body and mind. Horses selling for $15 in Seattle could easily bring $600 in the Yukon. A four-room apartment in that city rented for $1.25, while the cheapest, single, shabby room in Dawson cost $25 a week. A 40-cent quart of whiskey commanded a dollar and milk was five times the price of whiskey. Coffee normally selling for 13 cents a pound sold for 50 cents a cup. However, the American working man earned $1.25 a day, whereas a Dawson teamster earned $100.

A man's determination can best be measured by the extent to which he is willing to suffer. The lust for gold drove men to their limits and beyond. They endured blistered feet, running sores from the packs, frost-bitten faces skinned to raw flesh, snow blindness, crippling rheumatism, and — the most common killer — scurvy. With this disease the heart beats erratically, legs ache and go lame, flesh becomes soft, puffy and discolours blue to black, gums swell, teeth fall out and the eyes sink into the still-conscious "skeleton". Many men could not exist like this and found release in death or madness.

The Klondike created its own famous characters both in fiction and reality. The celebrated poet, Robert W. Service, although not taking part in the gold rush, described so vividly the personages Sam McGee, Dangerous Dan McGrew and the Lady known as Lou, that they have taken on lifelike images in our minds. The actual inhabitants of Dawson had equally exciting lives. Swiftwater Bill Gates repeatedly gained and lost both fortunes and women, only to die in an automobile accident in Seattle in 1943. Big Alex McDonald from Antigonish, Nova Scotia, became known as "The King of the Klondike". To him gold was trash and his only interest, the purchasing of property, eventually led to his ruin. The dancehall queen, Gertie Lovejoy, alias Diamond-Tooth Gertie, lives on in the name of one of Dawson's few remaining saloons.

From discovery to abandonment the Klondike gold rush lasted three years almost to the day. With the announcement of a fortune in gold dust in the sands of Nome, Alaska, eight thousand left Dawson within a week, leaving the valleys in peace again.

The Klondike rush merely repeats the history of man's lust for gold, lust that has been evident for thousands of years.

"I have given thee the gold countries"   (epistle from the Sun God, Temple of Edfu, Egypt, *c.* 1300 BC)

Archaeologists believe that native gold, because of its glitter, would have caught the eye of prehistoric man sooner than other, duller, native metals such as copper or silver. The first crude decorations of worked gold, found along the Nile Valley, date back to at least the fourth millenium BC, but lumps of native gold, used in their natural state, were valued before this time as amulets and charms.

In Canada little evidence exists of the prehistoric use of gold. Explorers came determined to find a wealth of gold in this new land but met with disappointment. This was the case for Frobisher in the 1570s, when he returned to England from Baffin Island with several tonnes of useless rock mistakenly thought to contain gold.

The Royal Bank Plaza, Toronto, has 2,500 oz
of pure 24 kt gold coating the glass exterior
panels. This highly reflective yet transparent
material, Polarpane, effectively reduces the
sun's heat in summer and saves it in winter.
Clive Webster.

Canada's earliest gold mines, such as those of the Chaudiere River region, Quebec, of 1847, and the Klondike, Yukon, of 1896, were in placer deposits. These deposits form when heavy, durable gold weathers from its parent rock and, because of its weight, is concentrated in a bed of sand and gravel by the action of a stream current. Placers can be mined by panning or through the use of sluice boxes. Both of these simple devices rely on water washing away the lightweight minerals to leave the heavy gold metal. Following the big rush in the Yukon, dredges handled most of the placer mining. Thirty-five of these monsters were built in the Yukon. The larger dredges could process up to fourteen thousand cubic metres of gravel in a twenty-four-hour day, recovering as much as eleven thousand grams of gold. The price of gold today has led to a revival of mining in the area. Large earth-movers can go higher in the valleys than can the dredges, bringing down vast quantities of material for sluicing out the gold. The added complication of permafrost requires many of the mining ventures to use high-pressure water jets to loosen the soil before it can be hauled. Most of the gold is recovered as fine particles and rarely as large nuggets. The world's largest nugget, found at Carson Hill, California, weighs 72.78 kilograms. The largest recorded Canadian gold nugget came from the Yukon and weighed 2.64 kilograms. The Klondike provided some of the richest placer deposits in the world in terms of percentage of gold contained within the gravels.

Since the end of the nineteenth century no major placer deposits have been found in Canada and gold is mined principally as fine-grained disseminations in rock. These lode deposits require the crushing of the ore to release the gold. Most of them are confined to the Canadian Shield in early Precambrian rocks that date back approximately two and one-half billion years. The principal gold camps of Porcupine, Kirkland/Larder Lake and northwestern Quebec have a recent addition; Hemlo in the Thunder Bay district. A considerable amount of gold is also recovered as a by-product of copper, zinc and nickel mining. Canada is the world's third largest producer of gold, following upon South Africa and the Soviet Union.

"Gold, man's first follie" (Pliny, AD 79)
In Dawson men had little regard for their own lives while pursuing the big find, but once having gained their riches they would willingly trade for a loaf of bread an equal weight of gold. Since gold has very limited uses, almost 90 per cent of our production feeds the markets for jewellery, coins and bullion bars.

Gold does, however, possess some very interesting qualities beyond the warm, yellow colour, glowing lustre and fine texture that so fires men. It is a rare metal; the estimated world's supply would occupy a cube measuring 15 metres on each side.

The most malleable of metals, gold can be hammered into a foil a thousand times thinner than a piece of paper and so thin that light passes through it. It is very ductile; a piece of gold the size of a man's thumb can be drawn into a wire that would stretch from Montreal to Toronto — some five hundred and fifty kilometres. Again, these properties are useful for decorative purposes to make threads for weaving and foils for plating over other metals. It is highly resistant to corrosion, which accounts for the excellent preservation of surviving ancient artifacts. Corrosion resistance coupled with rarity has meant that gold has been re-used continually since earliest times, resulting in the destruction of many important works, artifacts having been melted down to produce new articles. A present-day gold filling might three thousand years ago have been gold jewellery worn by an Egyptian Queen. Its rarity, demands for investment and decoration, and man's greed, assure gold a lasting high monetary value.

Diodorus Siculus, in the first century BC, commented that "nature herself makes it clear that the production of gold is laborious, the guarding of it difficult, the zest for it very great, and its use balanced between pleasure and pain".

3

Jade from the Cassiar Mountains British Columbia

Jade, the Jewel of Heaven

No single mineral, gem or rock has been attributed such a variety of powers and been used in such diverse ways as has jade. It has been used for medicinal purposes, as a form of monetary exchange, for adornment, and to make tools and weapons. It has formed a part of religious ceremony and it has mystical connotations.

The Aztecs believed it cured ailments of the groin and the kidneys. Upon observing this, Cortez termed the stone *piedra de ijada* (hence jade), which is Spanish for "stone of the loin". Over the years, different cultures claimed that this mineral could cure biliousness, alleviate disorders of the blood, check hemorrhages, calm the mind, enrich the spirit, nourish the bones and relieve heartburn, asthma and thirst.

Inuit hunters carried jade as a talisman to bring good fortune. A sect of Moslems kept jade on their persons for protection. For the Chinese this mineral possessed a creative force and so was used to fashion objects of worship representing the deities of Heaven, Earth and the Four Cardinal Points of Direction. Aztec ceremonies of sacrifice could not be executed without the presence of jade. The Maoris of New Zealand carved it into neck pendants of a rather menacing humanoid figure, *hei-tiki*, which was a talisman buried with its owner.

The rarity and usefulness of jade made it very valuable to the ancients. The Aztecs prized it more than gold, and to North American Indians a jade chisel was worth three slaves.

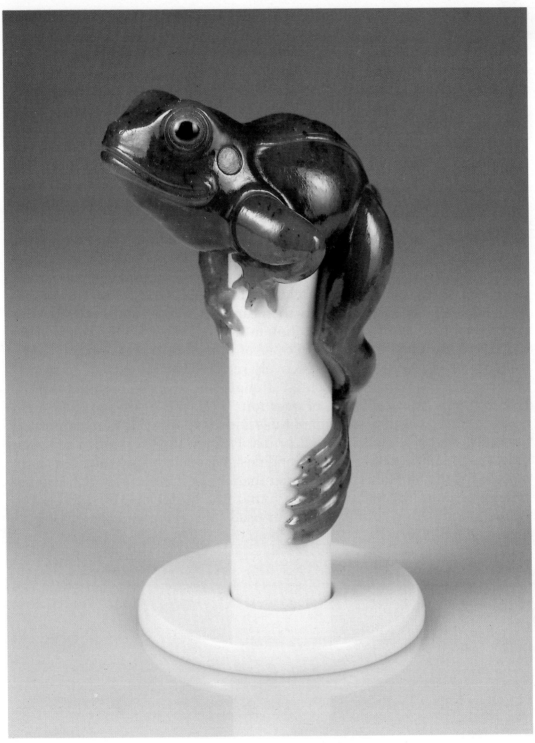

This modern carving, by Gerd Dreher, of
nephrite jade on a white chalcedony (quartz)
base copies an earlier work by Faberge.
J. Schekkerman.

Many cultures throughout history have admired the beauty of jade and have used it for decoration. The Inuit showed a fondness for the mineral in choosing translucent, green pieces as charms and for men's labrets; this jewellery buttoned through the lower lip and the inner disc rested against the gum to hold it securely in place. Later in the history of carving jade, the Chinese fashioned artifacts of leisure: a bed for the concubine of the emperor Huan-tsung (618-906), flutes, Ming (1368-1644) vases and screens, and the famous books of jade for the emperor Ch'ien-lung (1736-1796). Perhaps only Mugal or Indian jades surpassed these carvings. During the seventeenth and eighteenth centuries mastercarvers produced in jade such articles as dagger handles, teapots and thrones, often intricately inlaid with gold, rubies, sapphires, emeralds and diamonds.

The long and venerated history of jade is usually associated with the Chinese, but it has become apparent that the Indians along the northwest coast of North America were using jade in as early a period, if not earlier, than the Chinese. The Chinese refer to jade as *Yu*, which translates somewhat literally as beauty. Certainly their carvings, almost entirely decorative and ceremonial, reflect the veneration in which it was held. In contrast, the Salish Indians along the southern coast of British Columbia and the Tlingit Indians of the Alaska coast respectively referred to jade as "green stone" or "green". To them it represented strength and endurance, and from the time of their earliest artifacts of over four thousand years ago their main concern rested with the making of tools and weapons. The most important jade tool, the adze blade, served primarily for wood-working. The tough jade, shaped into a variety of sizes and designs, could be polished to a sharp chisel edge that remained keen longer than other stone implements. Sometimes a beautifully finished adze is found in a burial site. It would seem, from its sharp edge, that it was never used for carving and served only as a ceremonial object.

Inuit and Indian artifacts of nephrite jade.
Drill (smallest), adze, and chisel (largest).
Courtesy of Royal Ontario Museum, Toronto.

The Two Jade Minerals

Jade, a familiar word, is often misunderstood; for it is a term applied to several completely different minerals.

To the ancient carvers jade was a tough, green-coloured stone that suited their purposes for making tools and adornments. As the science of mineralogy developed, this material received the name tremolite. This particular variety of tremolite, commonly referred to as nephrite, consists of minute, feathery, interlocking crystals; which texture gives the mineral its toughness. The colour varies from light green, almost white, through shades of dark spinach-green to black. The darker colours result from an increase in the amount of iron in the tremolite.

During the eighteenth century the Chinese carvers discovered a jade mined in Burma. They soon realized that this material exhibited slightly better physical properties than did their usual jade. The "Burma jade", though still tough, differed in being harder, somewhat more brittle and a little heavier, and came in a greater variety of colours; shades of green, white, orange, brown, black, lilac and blue. They refined their carving skill to such a degree that the mottling of shades and hues highlighted and enhanced their works (a subtle technique today dormant). A century later, the French chemist Damour (1863) showed the essential difference between the two jades and named the rarer, Burmese one, jadeite. The most valued colour, an emerald green known as Imperial jade, may sell for several thousand dollars a carat.

Thus today there are two mineral species, tremolite and jadeite, that correctly describe the gemstone jade. Unfortunately, a number of inferior minerals resembling these are sold under trade names and one should beware of such terms as Manchurian jade, actually talc; Korean jade, the mineral serpentine; Indian jade, a mixture of green quartz and mica; American jade, or Californite, primarily grossular garnet and vesuvianite; and Mexican jade, a green-dyed marble. Although all these bear the name jade, they are not jade.

The Cassiar mine lies high on the side of
Mount McDame. Although essentially an
asbestos deposit, many tonnes of nephrite
jade are recovered annually. *Geological Survey
of Canada.*

B.C. Jade

Most of the jade seen in North America comes from British Columbia, hence the colloquial term B.C. jade. To date only tremolite has been found, but geological areas suitable for jadeite formation exist in the area. The tremolite jade, found in serpentine asbestos deposits, was formed under pressure at the time the Cordilleran Mountains pushed up along the west side of the Continent.

Today three principal areas in British Columbia mine jade; the Fraser River valley in the south, the central Omineca Mountains and the Cassiar Mountains to the north. Minor amounts of jade exist in the Yukon, but at present there is no active prospecting for the mineral there.

No doubt the Salish Indians collected jade in the form of waterworn alluvial boulders along the sand bars of the Fraser River. Their size and shape could be readily worked into the tools and weapons they needed. During the gold rush years, between 1850 and 1900, Chinese placer miners recognized this jade in their diggings and shipped many tonnes to China for carving. Today, mining jade from hard rock has gained in importance over the working of alluvial deposits. In the Cassiar district extensive deposits at the Cassiar mine, Dease Lake and Cry Lake are producing jade.

Annual export averages around five hundred tonnes, with the largest demand coming from Taiwan, Hong Kong and the Peoples Republic of China. In Canada the requirements of hobbyists and professional carvers are growing. The retail price varies with quality from a few dollars to $50 a kilogram. Good quality jade has a distinct grass-green colour, few fractures and a limited number of inclusions of black magnetite or softer minerals such as talc and chlorite. The jade story in Canada, although an old one, still unfolds. Each year new finds of this mineral raise interest around the world, for all men seem to have a need for this mystical gem.

Confucius (551 to 479 BC) likened the qualities of superior men to the excellence of jade:

> Soft and smooth yet gleaming, like benevolence;
> Fine, compact and strong, like intelligence;
> Unyielding yet not sharp and cutting, like righteousness;
> Its flaws never conceal its beauty nor does its beauty
> hide its flaw, like loyalty;
> And it is esteemed by all under the light of the sun,
> like the path of trust and duty.

4
Unexpected Treasures from Rapid Creek, Yukon Territory

The Mackenzie Delta, covering thousands of square kilometres, is named in honour of Alexander Mackenzie, who first explored the area in 1789. On the western horizon rises the scarp of the Richardson Mountains. *George Hunter, Masterfile.*

Drawn by Capt. Back R.N.

Mount Fitton   Richardson's Chain   The Barn Mountains

In 1826 Franklin, with his boats *Lion* and *Reliance*, charted the arctic coastline from Mackenzie River to Point Beechley. A thorough man, he collected geological specimens including ''rock-crystal'' (quartz), ''lydian stone'' (dark, fine-grained quartz) and ''grauwacke-slate used by the Esquimaux as a whet-stone''. Drawing by Captain Back showing the mouth of Blow River. *Public Archives Canada.*

The Arctic, Canada's final frontier, offers prospectors huge areas of potential mineral reserves. The area lay undisturbed by explorers until 1789 when Alexander Mackenzie appeared with his voyageurs and Indians. Leaving Great Slave Lake in late June they canoed down the river now bearing his name and paddled into the Arctic Ocean about two weeks later.

Two hundred kilometres from this ocean the Mackenzie River spreads out into a delta covering thousands of square kilometres. Many of the innumerable lakes and meandering channels lead nowhere. The marshlands abound with greyling, trout, ducks, moose and the inevitable hoards of mosquitoes and blackflies. The delta supports a number of Inuit fishermen and occasionally one spies a hut secreted in a remote part of this vast wilderness.

The natives of this area located their village, Aklavik, in the western portion of the area on a main channel leading to the sea. This provided them with ready access to the best fishing and hunting grounds. In 1964 the Diefenbaker Government decided this site was unsuitable. So it created Inuvik, complete with the airstrip, which ''modern man'' seems so desperately to require.

To the west the Richardson Mountains rise abruptly above the flat, featureless plain of the Mackenzie Delta. These mountains form a remarkable scarp over seven hundred metres in height. This far north the Richardson Mountains are not rugged but rounded, with river gorges cutting deeply into the gentle landscape. The upland tundra vegetation comprises grasses, sedges, lichens, mosses, dwarf birches and willows. Caribou, grizzly bear, wolf, bald eagle and the prevalent Richardson ground squirrel still roam this secluded land.

Lazulite, ''Gemstone'' of the Yukon

During the summer of 1959 Bruce Cameron, a geologist working for Triad Oil Company, collected a few blue, water-worn, mineral chips while conducting an oil exploration programme in the Blow River area of northeastern Yukon. Researchers identified the beautiful, azure-blue mineral as lazulite, a very rare magnesium aluminum hydrous phosphate.

Fifteen years after this, while prospecting for iron, Al Kulan stumbled onto the lazulite source along Rapid Creek. At the same time he collected a number of other odd-looking crystals, which his business partner, Gunar Penikis, sent to the Royal Ontario Museum, Toronto for identification. Curators Joe Mandarino and Darko Sturman reported these specimens as extremely fine examples of rare phosphate minerals, some of which were new discoveries in the mineral ''kingdom''.

Although the iron occurrences proved uneconomical for mining at the time, the efforts of Kulan and Penikis were not wasted. Good crystals of lazulite are rare, occurring at only a few other localities in the world, notably Austria, Sweden, Brazil and the United States. On 16 February 1976 the Commissioner of the Yukon declared lazulite the official gemstone of the Yukon Territory; hopefully a legislation that will protect this natural resource from excessive prospecting.

Gemstones are usually cut and polished, but lazulite proves too soft for fashioning. Yet a good specimen of this mineral fetches a high price because of its rarity and beauty. However, the lazulite, now widely distributed throughout the world, attracts less attention from collectors than do some of the later discoveries.

Beautiful octahedral crystals of wardite excel any in the world. The rare phosphate arrojadite, previously found only as ugly masses, occurs as excellent crystals on a ridge just above Rapid Creek. Similarly, collinsite, kryzhanovskite and whiteite had been found only as grains and crusts in remote reaches of the world until the work of Kulan and Penikis unearthed amazing specimens of these minerals in the Yukon.

The efforts of Alan Kulan and Gunar Penikis in discovering and developing this mineral occurrence received acknowledgment with the dedication of two new mineral species: kulanite and penikisite. Unfortunately, neither man lived long after the bestowal of this honour: Penikis died after a long and tragic illness while Kulan met a violent death in his home town of Ross River, Yukon.

The Naming of Minerals

Rapid Creek, a locality known for ten new mineral species, provides an excellent example of how the type of specimen must be described and named in order to be accepted and recognized by scientists throughout the world. Nahpoite, rapidcreekite, kulanite and penikisite represent minerals found, researched, named and first described from this area.

Two contrasting tendencies exist in mineralogical nomenclature: rational naming and irrational naming. Many of the early mineralogical names derive from Greek or Latin. Examples of minerals from Rapid Creek with names derived from the Greek are: pyrite from *pyr* meaning fire, referring to the sparks made when struck by steel; augelite from *auge* for lustre, which describes its characteristic pearly lustre on cleavage faces; eosphorite from *eos-phoros* meaning dawn-bearing, in allusion to its pink or yellow colour; barite from *barys*, for heavy, which aptly describes its density. These names are considered rational because they convey information about the mineral's appearance or its physical properties.

Similarly, nahpoite, a rational name, relates information about the chemistry of this species: sodium, symbol Na; hydrogen, symbol H; and phosphate, symbol PO. The ending "ite" is derived from the greek word *lithos* meaning rock or stone and thus has become the standard ending for all mineral names.

The other category of nomenclature, irrational, conveys no information about the mineral but bears names of persons or institutions: kulanite and penikisite honour the original discoverers and claim holders of this occurrence, Messrs Alan Kulan and Gunar Penikis; wicksite is named after Dr Frederick John Wicks, a curator at the Royal Ontario Museum; and satterlyite gives recognition to the famous Canadian geologist Dr Jack Satterly.

Lazulite ''gemstone of the Yukon'', perched
on brown siderite. The crystal measures
4 mm across. *J. Schekkerman*.

Rapid Creek cuts through the dark-coloured
iron formation exposing layers containing
beautiful and interesting phosphate minerals.
NMNS.

Vivianite crystals, 1 cm long. *J. Schekkerman.*

A spray of gormanite (measuring 7 mm) on
brown siderite. The mineral name honours
Dr D.H. Gorman, Professor of Mineralogy,
University of Toronto. *J. Schekkerman*.

Octahedral crystals of wardite sprinkled with
brown eosphorite. Each crystal measures
approximately 1 cm. *J. Schekkerman.*

Since 1959 mineral nomenclature has been controlled by the International Mineralogical Association, Commission on New Minerals and Mineral Names. The Commission consists of one voting member from each country actively involved in mineralogical research. Scientists making a submission for a new species must include a complete set of measurements and observations on appearance, physical and optical properties, crystallography and chemical composition. At the same time the researcher should put forward a name for consideration. If both the data and name pass the vote, then the species designation becomes internationally accepted and may be published. Once the information reaches the literature the name must be used in a consistent manner throughout the world.

Curiously enough, one of the major deterrents in the development of the Rapid Creek iron deposits, the presence of phosphate minerals, has now become a focal point for many people with differing interests: hobbyists seek prize display specimens for their collections; mineral dealers eye this source of desirable, marketable items; scientists eagerly search for new species and theories of formation; and politicians argue the pros and cons of conservation and levels of government authority.

5
The Rock Candy Mine
A Lesson in Mineral Identification

The beautiful Monashee Mountains surround the Rock Candy mine. This valley, just W of Osoyoos, is noted for its wine industry. *John de Visser, Masterfile.*

The Rock Candy mine lies huddled in a valley of the Monashee Mountains, southern British Columbia. The mine operated from 1918 to 1929 producing fluorite, which was hauled out by pack animals and later by aerial tramway to a mill two miles away. At that time fluorite served as an important additive in the manufacture of steel.

Prospectors originally staked the Rock Candy mine for copper, only to discover later that the green-coloured mineral, resembling rock candy, contained no copper at all. They had simply misidentified fluorite. Even to those experienced prospectors, who must be credited with having found many of the major ore deposits of this country, mineral identification always posed a problem. Understandably, then, to the uninitiated, mineral identification appears quite mysterious. Each of over three thousand species in the mineral "kingdom" occurs in such a variety of shapes and colours that it seems an overwhelming task to differentiate one from another.

Beginners and amateurs aspiring to identify minerals should not despair. A well-equipped mineralogical laboratory houses optical and scanning electron microscopes for detailed physical and optical observations, an X-ray generator for measurements of structural units within mineral crystals, an electron microprobe and atomic absorption spectroscopic units for chemical analysis; but this complex and cumbersome equipment is used only for very detailed mineralogical studies. Simple powers of observation, developed through practice, a good mineral identification book (examples given in the Bibliography), a small magnifying lens and a pocket knife comprise the essential tools for identifying a large number of minerals. After all, only a few dozen minerals occur commonly and a good knowledge of two hundred species would satisfy the needs of a professional geologist.

Fluorite and barite, minerals common in the Rock Candy mine, provide good examples for a discussion on mineral identification techniques. Physical properties necessary for mineral recognition include form (crystal shape), colour, lustre, fracture, cleavage, hardness and density. Although the following few paragraphs will not train anyone to be a prospector, they should convey to readers some of the language and fundamentals of the mineral sciences.

This rhombic crystal of barite has a glassy
lustre and several good cleavage planes. The
rather large plate measures 5 cm.
J. Schekkerman.

Crystals

During the eighteenth century, Abbé René Just Haüy of France originated
the term "flowers of the kingdom", in reference to the much admired per-
fectly smooth faces, symmetry and delicacy of crystals. That minerals actually grow in this fashion first appeared difficult to comprehend. Using his
insight into the laws of nature Haüy showed how crystals consist of identical building blocks stacked in three dimensions. The shape of these building blocks, or unit cells, depends on the internal arrangement of atoms,
which in turn determines the external form and symmetry of the crystals.
The variations of form and growth give the impression of innumerable pos-
sibilities or habits, but the basic laws of crystallography limit the number
of crystal systems to six. Recognizing a mineral's form is important to its
identification.

Over 30,000 t of fluorite were mined at Rock
Candy. The octahedral crystal measures 4 cm
and displays a vitreous lustre; several good
cleavages are evident. *J. Schekkerman.*

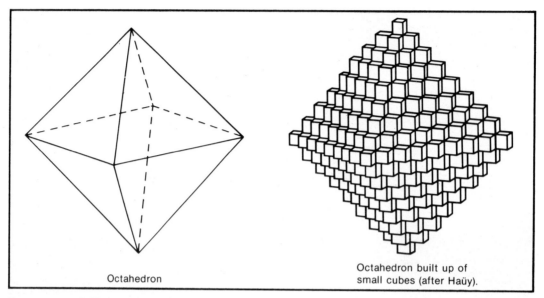

Octahedron

Octahedron built up of
small cubes (after Haüy).

Tout est trouvé. Hauy was the first to
recognize that crystals were composed of
identical building blocks. An octahedral
fluorite crystal may be constructed from a
large number of smaller, unit-cell cubes.

Colour and Lustre

Colour, although important aesthetically, is sometimes of little use in identification because small changes in chemistry can cause drastic alterations
to colour within a single mineral species. Fluorite when pure calcium fluoride, appears clear and colourless, but at the Rock Candy mine it is commonly a pale, sea-green and is sometimes colourless or purple. At other
localities shades of pink, yellow, blue, violet or black exist. Barite, barium
sulphate, usually a honey-yellow at the Rock Candy mine, may be found
as light grey or colourless crystals.

Minerals can be easily sorted into two broad categories based on lustre. Metallic lustre describes those that reflect light like a metal, nonmetallic
lustre denotes all others. Fluorite and barite, both nonmetallic, have a vitreous or glassy lustre and bright, shiny crystal faces. Other terms used to
describe the quality of reflected light include waxy, greasy, adamantine and
pearly.

A photograph of fluorite taken with the modern technology of a scanning electron microscope (magnified 50 times) shows Hauy's correct perception that an octahedral face is composed of stacked cubes. *NMNS.*

Cleavage and Hardness

All physical properties relate to a mineral's chemistry and atomic structure. Colour and lustre exemplify the chemistry while cleavage and hardness demonstrate directly some of the features of atomic bonding.

Within a crystal, atoms bond together by means of electrical forces of attraction. Along planes of weak bonding the mineral tends to break or cleave easily. This planar separation is called cleavage. Fluorite displays three perfect cleavages that outline an octahedron, while barite's three good cleavages break into lozenge-shaped prisms. If bond strengths are equivalent in all directions then the substance fractures into fragments like glass. A good example of this is the mineral quartz.

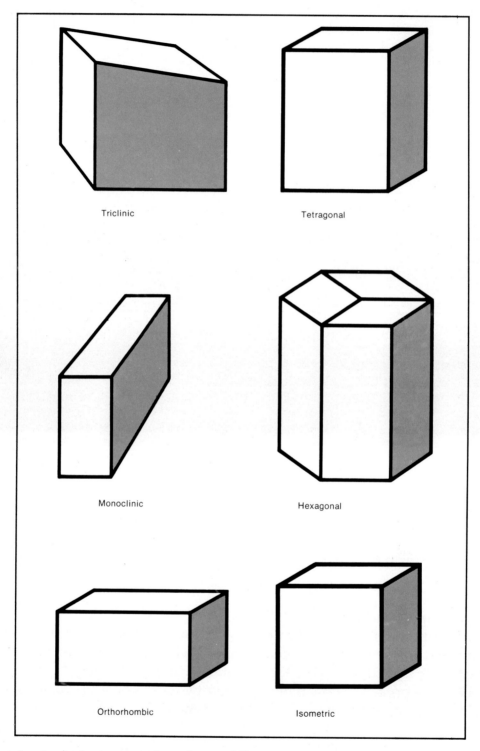

Triclinic

Tetragonal

Monoclinic

Hexagonal

Orthorhombic

Isometric

An atomic structure must have the possibility
of repeating itself *ad infinitum*. There are only
6 crystal systems that satisfy these conditions
of symmetry.

Hardness measures a mineral's resistance to scratching. The German mineralogist, Friedrich Mohs (1773-1839), arranged ten minerals in increasing order of hardness. This became known as Mohs scale of hardness; talc, the softest, is assigned one on the scale and diamond, the hardest, ten. Bearing in mind that a fingernail has a hardness of two and a pocket knife blade five and one-half, allows us to group minerals as soft, intermediate or hard depending on whether or not they can be scratched by a fingernail or a knife. This suffices for most identifications. In testing, however, never damage a beautiful part of the specimen.

Fluorite and barite can both be scratched by a knife but not by a fingernail, so their hardness falls between two and five and one-half. Fluorite (Mohs hardness four) scratches the softer barite (Mohs hardness three).

Density

Before attempting to lift an object, a person has a feeling of that object's weight. This "heft" has an exact scientific measurement, density, which measures the weight of a specified volume. A carton of books feels heavier than expected while foam cushions lift with surprising ease. This sensitivity to weight plays an important role in mineral identification.

Through practice one should be able to differentiate between minerals more or less dense than common quartz or feldspar, both of which have a density of 2.6 grams per cubic centimetre. Barite and fluorite, decidedly heavier, have densities of 4.5 and 3.2 respectively. Gold, the most dense mineral, measures 19 grams per cubic centimetre and ice, the least dense, 0.9 grams. It may be helpful to remember water's density of 1 gram per cubic centimetre.

The misidentification of the simple minerals of the Rock Candy mine seems difficult to comprehend, but in retrospect matters often appear so. The important lesson for all is never to take anything for granted and to make careful, routine observations with each identification to reduce the number of errors.

> Go, my sons, buy stout shoes, climb the mountains, search the valleys, the deserts, the sea shores, and the deep recesses of the earth. Mark well the various kinds of minerals, note their properties and their mode of origin.

> Petrus Severinus (1571)

6

Petrified Wood from the Dinosaur Graves of Southern Alberta

Badlands of Dinosaur Provincial Park
sculpted by the Red Deer River. *Geological
Survey of Canada.*

The feeling of comfort and leisure when crossing the flat, lush prairies quickly disappears on descending into the Red Deer River valley. The river cuts the sedimentary layers of beige, grey and black outlined in burgundy and terra cotta into fantastic shapes of domes, hoodoos and incised coulées. The meandering river has cut a broad valley with deep, rilled banks. The canyon floor, sparsely vegetated by small cactus, some grass and cottonwoods, leaves a barren, dusty, semidesert. This alien world lends itself to the imagining of giant beasts sounding their challenge for battle. Yet these badlands of today in no way resemble the landscape roamed by dinosaurs seventy million years ago.

A vast, shallow sea extending from the present-day Gulf of Mexico to the Arctic Ocean inundated much of what is now Great Plains. Drumheller and Dinosaur Provincial Park are situated on the former western coastal plain of this sea. Here the steaming deltas and marshes supported stands of bald-cypress, sycamore, China fir and dawn redwood. Swamps infested with crocodiles, duckbilled dinosaurs and huge lizards became burial grounds for plants and animals alike, sediment (eroded from the mountains to the west) quickly covering their remains in thick layers of mud. These buried remains form the dinosaur bone beds, coal seams and petrified wood of today, and are exposed only where the Red Deer River has cut through the overlying sandstones.

In 1884 Joseph Burr Tyrrell, while mapping the geology of the Red Deer River valley, discovered the first dinosaur skull near Drumheller. Since then palaeontologists have excavated hundreds of skeletons, studied the geology and made interpretations of life during the Upper Cretaceous period. Near the original discovery site the new Tyrrell Museum commemorates his find.

Petrified wood (larger piece measures 11 cm)
replaced by quartz. Logs up to 15 m long
and stumps 2 m in diameter have been
found. *J. Schekkerman*.

Petrified Wood: a Plant Fossil

Redwood and bald-cypress were abundant in the sultry environment of the ancient Drumheller area. Trees swept into the murky waters were quickly swallowed by mud, which prevented rotting. Over a period of millions of years great accumulations of sediments buried the trees. The ground water in these sediments contained dissolved minerals. The wood fibre soaked up the solution and the minerals replaced the tissue of the plant, preserving the details of the cellular fabric so faithfully in stone, that today palaeo-botanists can often identify the tree species. This petrified wood is only exposed today after a long period of erosion of the covering sedimentary rocks. The most prized specimens of petrified wood are those replaced by quartz, a very hard mineral that withstands the action of erosion that originally released it from the surrounding sediments. When a softer mineral like calcite replaces the wood much of the detail and beauty of the structure disappears.

Only rarely, does quartz (silica) replace the dinosaur bones, and these silicified remains are darker, heavier and tougher than those impregnated with calcite. These prized remains, as all fossils, are protected by Albertan law against illegal collecting without a permit. As the Red Deer releases these remains from their graves, palaeontologists painstakingly gather them to expand their work on the interpretation of former life on our planet.

7

Esterhazy, Saskatchewan
A Mineral Source to Save the World

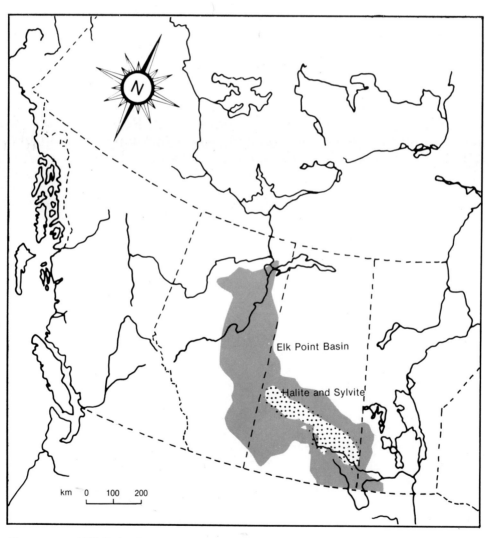

The extent of Elk Point Basin 400,000,000
years ago and its salt and potash deposits
(dotted).

The Marietta Miner, a 4-rotor continuous boring machine, has 4 cutting heads that can mine more than 10.8 t of ore per minute. It sweeps out a path 7.9 m wide and 1.4 m high. *Cominco Ltd., Vancouver.*

Food remains man's most basic need. Southern Saskatchewan provided arable land, vital to existence for both the Paleo-Indian of twelve thousand years ago and the European immigrant of more recent date. Lately, oil exploration has revealed potash deep beneath the lush prairie. Now this area not only supplies large crops of grain but, coincidentally, holds a mineral resource capable of increasing crop yields elsewhere around the world.

Saskatchewan Potash: an Evaporite Formation

Four hundred million years ago a sea covered northern Montana and North Dakota, southern Saskatchewan, north-central Alberta and a small portion of the southern part of the Northwest Territories. Slowly a reef grew across the northern strait, segregating this extensive sea from the open ocean. This barrier restricted the supply of oceanic water and the warm, dry climate gradually evaporated the water leaving behind a vast residue of salts, much like that presently forming at Great Salt Lake, Utah. These mineral salts consist mainly of halite, or common salt (sodium chloride), and anhydrite (calcium sulphate). The relatively thin layers of sylvite (potassium chloride) precipitated when the salinity of the sea water reached its maximum. These sylvite layers constitute the high-grade potash ore of southern Saskatchewan.

During millions of years, sediments laid down in seas or eroded from the western mountains and deposited across the interior region buried the evaporites, and the recent rich, dark prairie soil formed on the surface.

During the oil exploration programme of the 1940s no great gusher spouted forth. However, an extensive potash deposit was outlined six hundred kilometres long and eighty kilometres wide. But the formation containing the potash beds lay a thousand metres below the surface of the prairie. Individual beds of ore may not even reach a metre in thickness, but the huge lode, of over four million tonnes, warranted consideration, for it has long been known in Europe and North America that potash makes crops grow better.

Potash, an old word, derives from the early production of potassium salts obtained by boiling wood ashes and water in a large pot. The white residue, pot ash, was dumped on crops to help their growth. Early North American Indians made similar observations and used ashes and fish to fertilize their fields of corn. Today agriculture consumes 95 per cent of Canadian potash production. The essential element, potassium, improves root and fibre growth as well as plant food production.

Potash ore from the mines of Saskatchewan essentially contains 3 minerals: milky-white sylvite (potassium chloride); clear, colourless halite (sodium chloride) and red-coloured clay. Width of field of view is about 4 cm. *J. Schekkerman.*

The potash mine shaft, mill and cone-shaped
storage bins of the International Minerals &
Chemical Corp. (Canada) Ltd., near
Esterhazy. *Energy, Mines and Resources.*

Esterhazy and the Mining Challenge

"Count" Paul Oscar Esterhazy (1831-1912) dedicated his life to saving his
Hungarian compatriots from the political unrest prevailing after 1867.
Perhaps his erect lean appearance was his only claim to aristocracy, but his
leadership qualities proved undeniable. In 1886 his vision guided thirty-five
families past the temptations and unhealthy atmosphere of the Pennsylva-
nian mines and foundries all the way out to the Esterhazy Colony in southern
Saskatchewan. This paradise of green, rolling hills bounded to the south
by the Qu'Appelle River valley, resembled their homeland. For $10 these
hardy families could purchase 160 acres of fertile land and, pleased with
their freedom in New Hungary, they worked hard and learned to endure
the severe winters. Persistence became the guiding word for this community.

Every mining venture provides a challenge. In the case of the potash
deposits of southern Saskatchewan, reaching the ore proved expensive and
hazardous.

The first shaft, about eleven kilometres northeast of Esterhazy, took five years and ten million dollars for International Minerals and Chemical Corporation (Canada) Limited to sink, arriving at potash level on 8 June 1962. Even to start the shaft required installing huge refrigeration plants to freeze the water-laden clay, sand and boulders of the top 90 metres. A brine solution of $-20°$ Celsius pumped down drill holes froze this layer, making it possible to dig it out and line the cavity with concrete before the layer had time to thaw out. The next 300 metres of shaft-sinking proceeded routinely with blasting and mucking; then the dreaded Blairmore layer was reached. This most obstinate stratum required two and one-half years to defeat. It consisted of a 60-metre layer of liquid quicksand under explosive pressures, as high as 1,100 pounds per square inch (seven mega Pascals). Miners working at $-35°$ Celsius removed 2-metre sections at a time and collared the shaft with over forty tonnes of cast iron. Once below the Blairmore another ten rivers had to be plugged with two hundred thousand bags of cement. At pressures 1,030 metres below the surface, salt behaves like plastic, sealing out water. Again, perseverance assured the success of IMC, the miners and the people of Esterhazy, and the ore could be mined.

The continuous miner wields two or four huge rotary heads which chew out a tunnel of potash-bearing salt. The ore conveyed on belts to the shaft is hoisted to the mill. Milling begins by crushing and sieving the ore to a suitable size. The useful sylvite separates from common salt in flotation cells much like those described in Chapter 12, Sudbury. The final product when dried consists of approximately 95 per cent pure sylvite or potash.

Following the success of Esterhazy, mines opened up across the province, making Canada the world's largest exporter of potash. Seventy per cent of the production goes to the United States and the remainder is largely purchased by Japan, China, India, Brazil and Korea.

8
Gypsum Rosettes from the Red River Floodway, Manitoba

The Red River Floodway barely indents the
plane of sediments left behind by glacial Lake
Agassiz. It is empty for most of the year but
in spring it serves its purpose well;
preventing annual flooding of Winnipeg. *John
de Visser, Masterfile.*

Lake Agassiz: Legacy of An Ice Age

Some 12,300 years ago the Wisconsinan ice sheet began its final, silent retreat north, signalling the end of the last great ice age. As the glacier melted, an enormous body of fresh water inundated the plains. During the five-thousand-year history of this lake, Agassiz, it submerged a total of 950,000 square kilometres at various times. Its western shore attracted the woolly mammoth and mastodon. The gradual warming climate replaced the pine and spruce forests with the grasslands we are familiar with today. Huge bison herds roamed these prairies, hunted by the Paleo-Indian as long as ten thousand years ago.

Lake Agassiz reached its maximum extent about 9,500 years ago. At this point in its history the waters burst through the eastern margins of the ice sheet into Lake Superior, catastrophically lowering the Lake Agassiz level. Further retreat of the glacier into the Hudson Bay Lowlands marked the final lake era as it drained north into the Tyrrell Sea 7,500 years ago.

The enormous weight of the ice ground the rock over which it moved. As the ice flow melted, the rock particles imbedded in it were deposited as mud on the bottom of the lake. In the area of present-day Winnipeg, Lake Agassiz attained a depth of over two hundred metres with an accumulation of approximately twenty metres of clay-rich sediments.

Crystals Grow

> Socrates discusses how far a flea can jump, we discuss why snowflakes, when they first fall, always have six corners and six projections, tufted like feathers.
>
> J. Kepler (1611)

The flat, sedimentary plane of southern Manitoba, a remnant of Lake Agassiz, does not appear a likely place to find minerals, yet during the excavation of the Red River Floodway, in the early 1950s, beautiful rosettes of the mineral gypsum were exposed in the clay sediments some five metres below the ground level of the prairie.

How do these rosettes exist in a fine-grained sediment formed by the grinding action of a glacier and subsequently deposited in a lake of meltwater? The answer is simple: they grew there after the sediments formed. Now, how do crystals grow?

A rosette of gypsum crystals (8 cm across)
found in the muds of the Red River
Floodway. *J. Schekkerman.*

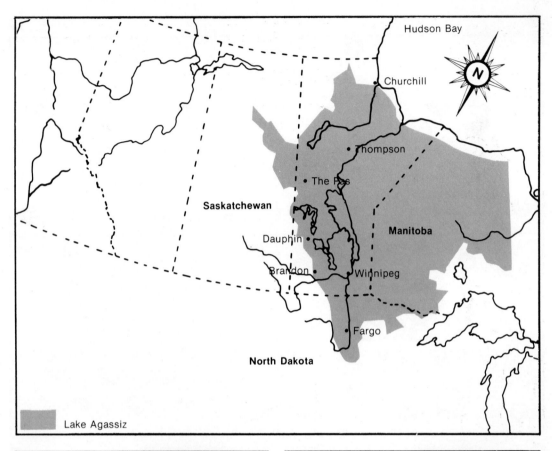

Lake Agassiz

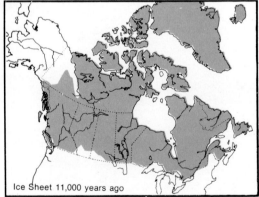

Ice Sheet 11,000 years ago

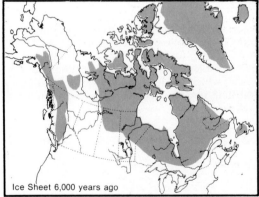

Ice Sheet 6,000 years ago

Total area covered by glacial Lake Agassiz
from about 12,000 to 7,000 years ago, and the
ice sheets 11,000 and 6,000 years ago.

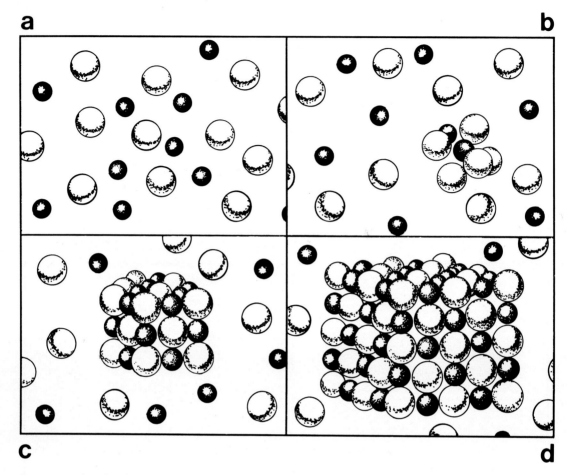

Sequence of 4 sketches illustrating sodium
atoms (small circles) and chlorine atoms
(large circles): (a) in a solution; (b) forming a
seed halite (sodium chloride or common salt)
crystal, which gradually grows; (c,d) as more
atoms are removed from solution and bonded
to its surface.

Minerals consist of crystals that are a regular arrangement of atoms. A growing crystal does not draw its nourishment from within as an animal does. It must grow from outside — from material presented to its surface. This material must contain the right chemical elements, free to arrange themselves correctly in the crystal structure.

The gypsum crystals found in the Red River Floodway sediments grew from a water solution that contained singular, electrically charged particles, or ions, of calcium and sulphate. The calcium, sulphate and water combined at the surface of the crystals, each ion adopting a particular position, dictated by the electrical forces of attraction acting upon it. Settling into these positions the orderliness of the structure extended and the gypsum crystals grew.

This book contains numerous photographs of natural crystals; minerals, that have grown from solutions and molten rock. Today the production of man-made or synthetic crystals has become increasingly more important: they form a part of ''solid state'' components of hearing aids, auto ignitions, radios and computers; and are used as synthetic gems, ''jewels'' in watches; and lasers. The reader, equipped with a few chemicals and a book of instructions, may thrill to the experience of growing his own crystals. In the controlled atmosphere of a laboratory or at home, crystals can grow quite quickly; several millimetres a day. Even at the modest growth rate of a millimetre a day it requires approximately a hundred layers of atoms per second to organize themselves; try to imagine the hustle and bustle of atoms as they arrange themselves in this perfect order. In nature, growth conditions never occur so ideally — it probably takes several years to grow a gypsum crystal in the clays of ancient Lake Agassiz. Still, nature has time.

9
Bernic Lake, Manitoba
Mining for Space-age Elements

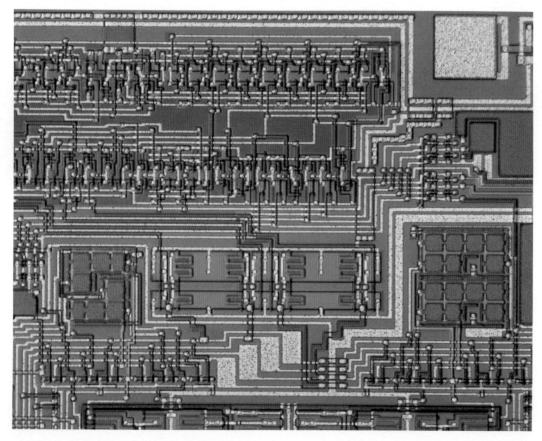

The Bernic Lake mine contains a considerable amount of beryllium, an element essential in the manufacture of high-tech microelectronics. The intricate labyrinth of electronic circuitry is emplaced on a heat-resistant beryllium oxide base (magnified 50 times). *Hans Blohm, Masterfile.*

Nestled in the forests of southeastern Manitoba lies the small, neat, mining operation of Tanco. The mine, with its headframe on the shores of Bernic Lake has a more attractive appearance than most mines, but to the casual passer-by it resembles scenes common in many parts of Canada.

Yet this deposit holds a surprise. It contains significant concentrations of minerals with rare elements, making it one of the world's largest supplies of tantalum, lithium, beryllium, cesium, rubidium and gallium. Their applications, often still in the innovatory and development stages, sound like the technical list from a Star Wars movie; rockets, magneto hydrodynamic generators, lasers, computers and nuclear reactors. Farsighted and venturesome men have dared to invest in this mine.

For many years the Tanco Corporation has been mining wodginite (manganese-tin-tantalum oxide) and maganotantalite (manganese-tantalum oxide). Tantalum, recovered from these minerals, has unique properties of high density, good electrical conductivity, high melting point and resistance to corrosion. This combination ideally suits jet engine turbine blades, nuclear-reactor radiation shielding and electrolytic capacitors for heart pacemakers.

Lithium, the lightest solid element, can be alloyed with aluminum to give a lighter, stronger metal, which the RA-5C Vigilante — a military jet capable of speeds up to Mach 2 — successfully demonstrates. Lithium has become a household word to thousands of people since its application as a drug for the treatment of manic-depressive illness, drug abuse, paranoia and schizophrenia.

At Bernic Lake, lepidolite, petalite and spodumene comprise the most common lithium-bearing minerals. Most of the petalite and spodumene could be providing the raw materials in the production of cookware such as Corningware and Vision, however, it is possible that some of the lithium from these minerals is being used in the revolutionary, lightweight storage batteries such as have hitherto successfully powered cars. Potentially this mode of energy could provide emission-free engines with lower maintenance costs.

Considerable amounts of beryl occur in the Bernic Lake deposit. Although, unfortunately, none of the beautiful gem varieties such as aquamarine, emerald or morganite exist here, the beryl still serves as a potential source of the metal beryllium. Neutrons hazardous to health miraculously rebound off this metal thus remaining within the core of nuclear reactors. Its lightweight, exceptional hardness and resistance to high temperatures yield a material for rocket and missile construction. A somewhat less exotic but equally useful material results when beryllium is alloyed with copper; a unique hard, non-sparking metal. Beryllium-copper wrenches and hammers, especially designed for work adjacent to fuel tanks, may be used without fear of causing an explosion.

Cesium, the most reactive of all metals, burns immediately on exposure to oxygen. Its burn, several times hotter than that of propane, produces a sufficiently high temperature to form an ionized gas or plasma. When the plasma interacts with a magnetic field, it generates electricity. This safe power source, a magnetohydrodynamic generator, has no moving mechanical parts to wear out and its efficiency and output capacity can be increased simply with a larger volume of gas. Such power generators, although only in the experimental stages, may prove an efficient alternative to fossil-fuelled steam or nuclear generators. Future developments in space travel will probably involve cesium-fuel ion engines. Miners at Tanco stockpile pollucite, a cesium-aluminum silicate, as an ore of future importance.

Pegmatites: the Final Stage

On reducing our scope to the thin crust of the earth we observe that animals, plants and water become an insignificant, fragile unstable content of our planet. Eight chemical elements comprise about 99 per cent of the crust's weight: oxygen 46.6 per cent, silicon 27.7, aluminum 8.1, iron 5.0, calcium 3.6, sodium 2.8, potassium 2.6 and magnesium 2.1. These elements combine to form the most abundant minerals and mineral groups; feldspar, quartz, mica, amphibole and pyroxene. Why then do the rare elements of the Tanco mine occur in one limited space?

The Bernic lake deposit lies in a body of rock called a pegmatite. Most pegmatites result from the last stage of a lengthy sequence of crystallization from an igneous magma or molten rock. As minerals separate, the remaining liquid becomes enriched in volatile components such as water and fluorine. This highly mobile fluid escapes from the magma chamber into the surrounding rocks, carrying with it all the elements that, because of their atomic size, cannot find a place in the crystal structures of the common rock-forming minerals. Included are the small atoms of the light elements beryllium and lithium and the large-sized, heavy atoms of cesium, rubidium, gallium and tantalum. From this watery magma the pegmatite crystallizes, consisting primarily of large blocky crystals of feldspar, mica and quartz. Once again the rare elements listed above cannot find a place in the crystal structure of these common minerals. They remain and concentrate in the liquid magma, crystallizing only at the very end. For this reason these rare constituents reside together in a limited volume and form an economic deposit.

The Tanco mine will cease to operate soon. With the equipment removed, the excavated caverns will be left to quiet darkness and eventual flooding. The depletion of tantalum reserves marks the end of this mining period. Its reopening depends on man's needs, advances in technology and the feasibility of economic mining.

10

Amethyst from Thunder Bay, Ontario
An Ancient Amulet

The deep, rich, purple of amethyst has attracted wearers for six thousand years and still competes as one of the most popular gemstones. In addition to its desirable colour it is associated with a multitude of powers and myths. Traditionally the amethyst preserves its bearer from drunkenness; but those wishing to test its sobering effects should heed the ancient writers' admission that water served in a vessel made of this purplish stone gave the appearance of wine, yet could be consumed in any quantity without inebriation. While casting doubt on the powers of this amulet, dedicated believers expanded the lore associated with amethyst to include the preservation of soldiers in battle, assistance to hunters in capturing game and protection from contagion.

The amethyst assumed a religious symbolism as well. In the Old Testament, the Book of Exodus describes the breastplate of the high-priest Aaron (*c.* 1300 BC) as containing twelve gems; red jasper, light-green serpentine, green feldspar, garnet, lapis lazuli, onyx, brown agate, banded agate, amethyst, yellow jasper, malachite and jade or green jasper. The Hebrew name for amethyst, *halom,* means the stone that induces dreams and visions. The Rosicrucians, who combined both pagan and Christian ritual, believed that the amethystine colour represented sacrifice, a symbol of love, passion, suffering and hope. In the Christian faith a St Valentine's legend mentions an amethyst ring with an engraving of Cupid. This reference to St Valentine's may be questionable, but does bear semblance to present-day customs.

Similarly, the lore of amethyst today signifies it as the eighth hour of the day, Wednesday in the week, the seventeenth wedding anniversary and the birthstone of February. It falls under the influence of the planet Jupiter and the zodiac sign of Pisces.

> From passion and from care kept free
> Shall Pisces' children ever be
> Who wear so all the world may see
> the amethyst.

Surindro Mohun Tagore

Amethyst, Ontario's Gemstone

On 14 May 1975 the Honourable Leo Bernier, Minister of Natural Resources, proclaimed amethyst the official mineral of Ontario in recognition of its beauty and historical importance.

These terminated amethyst crystals, each approximately 1 cm in width, display the beauty of "Ontario's Gemstone".
J. Schekkerman.

The only significant occurrence of amethyst in Ontario lies north of Lake Superior, east of Thunder Bay. The French explorers Radisson and Groseilliers referred to the locality in 1662. Sir William Logan, first Director of the Geological Survey of Canada and the National Museum of Canada, gave a geological report on the area of 1846. Shortly after this the McEachern brothers (Duncan, Malcolm and Edward) began mining amethyst. In the fall of 1862 they loaded two tonnes of stone into a small boat and sailed to Toronto. Docking at the small city's wharf they peddled their wares throughout the winter. Much to the vendors' pleasure, sales of amethyst exceeded their expectations, largely because of its novelty. Similar success met shipments to Montreal, Niagara Falls and Pike's Peak. Then, with the discoveries of higher quality, less expensive material in Brazil, interest in the Thunder Bay deposits rapidly declined. A hundred-year lull for Canadian amethyst followed this event.

Today, renewed interest in Ontario amethyst has resulted in the activity in two mines (Thunder Bay Amethyst and the Diamond Willow), with several others operating more sporadically. Good amethyst crystal groups, carefully collected to prevent damage, provide highly-prized display specimens. Crystal groups can measure up to a metre across with single crystals measuring fifteen centimetres in diameter and having pyramidal terminations of the same order of magnitude. Points of some crystals facet clean gems, while much of the amethyst, freed of associated rock, yields an excellent source of jewellery material either as cabochons or free-form tumbled stones. For the Thunder Bay mines by far the largest market is for the amethystine rock. Quarried blocks of granite, showing some amethyst, are used for facing buildings, as landscaping stone and for bookends.

The exploitation of Thunder Bay amethyst has just begun. Potentially large reserves exist for good construction grade and there are minor amounts of gem grade. Beautiful display specimens should be readily available for the careful collector.

The Origin of Thunder Bay Amethyst
Bacchus, the god of wine, angered by a slight to his person, vowed vengeance on the next individual his procession passed. His wrath fell upon Amethyst, a beautiful maiden travelling to worship at the shrine. Bacchus released his vicious tigers on the helpless girl, but the goddess Diana spared Amethyst a cruel death by transforming her into a pure white, stone statue. Recognizing the miracle and repenting his cruelty, Bacchus poured an offering of grape wine over the figure, turning it a deep purple colour.

The shores of Lake Superior wash the
ancient Precambrian rocks that constitute this
rough terrain of NW Ontario. *Hans Blohm,
Masterfile.*

This myth hardly provides a scientific explanation for the origin of amethyst but it does suggest an interesting source for its colour. The mineral quartz, as pure silicon dioxide, appears colourless or white. Amethyst, a coloured variety of quartz, contains minor chemical impurities of iron in the crystal structure that colour it shades of purple and the less desirable red-brown. In the past, the great demand for this gemstone resulted in the production of a number of substitutes such as amethyst-coloured garnet, corundum and glass. Today manufacturers produce quartz of any colour in large quantities. This readily available synthetic amethyst can only be differentiated from the natural mineral with experienced skill.

The amethyst localities north of Lake Superior lie within a band some forty kilometres wide, beginning approximately sixty kilometres northeast of the city of Thunder Bay and extending about two hundred kilometres east to Rossport. Early Precambrian rocks comprise the geology of this area. These ancient rocks, two and a half billion years old, folded and fractured into a breccia, leaving open channels that were ascended by deep, warm-water solutions. As these solutions rose and cooled, amethyst crystals ''seeded'' and grew. The resulting fine-grained blocks of granitic rock, cemented together with purple amethyst, attract the eye. In some cases fissures not entirely filled, left cavities encrusted with sharply terminated crystals.

Whether or not you believe in the mystic powers of amethyst as the present-day Ayurvedics do, its sacred and royal lineage attests to its success. For this reason amethyst, scraped from little pockets deep in the bush of Thunder Bay, has circulated throughout the world. Neither time nor the invention of synthetics has decreased the demand for this gem.

11
The MacLeod Iron Mine, Ontario

Ojibwan Land of the ''Wild Goose'' — Wawa
The early European explorers Jacques Cartier and Samuel de Champlain listened with avarice to the Indians' tales of the wealth found to the west. In 1617 Champlain dispatched Etienne Brûlé to explore the Western Seas for a mysterious ''floating isle'' laden with copper. Michipicoten Island, named by the Ojibwa for its impressive bluffs and protected by the evil spirit Missibize and the deity Nanibozhoo, evaded the greedy fingers of Brûlé, who returned only with pieces of copper given him by the Indians. Whether it was the guarding spirits or the fierce Iroquois themselves, the land of Michipicoten remained the hunting grounds of the Indians and venturesome coureurs-de-bois for almost three more centuries.

Like many of the mineral deposits discovered in Canada, it was the lure of gold that brought prospectors north of Lake Superior. In 1898, during the first gold rush in the area, Ben Boyer and Jim Sayers staked a rich deposit of iron ore just north of Wawa Lake, which developed into the Helen Iron mine. Surviving several name changes, the Helen still operates today as the MacLeod.

The Wawa deposit contains several iron-bearing minerals; hematite (iron oxide), goethite (hydrated iron oxide), siderite (iron carbonate), pyrite (iron sulphide) and marcasite (iron sulphide). The most common iron-ore minerals combine oxygen and iron. Iron also combines with sulphur, and although the minerals formed could be used as a source of iron, they are not actively mined today since not only do the oxides contain a higher percentage of iron metal but the smelting of sulphides results in problems with noxious sulphur gases.

Mineral	Chemical composition	% Iron (Fe)
Native iron	Fe (iron)	100
Magnetite	Fe_3O_4 (iron oxide)	72
Hematite	Fe_2O_3 (iron oxide)	70
Goethite	FeO(OH) (hydrated iron ixode)	63
Pyrrhotite	$Fe_{1-x}S$ (iron sulphide)	60
Siderite	$FeCO_3$ (iron carbonate)	48
Pyrite	FeS_2 (iron sulphide)	47
Marcasite	FeS_2 (iron sulphide)	47

Between 1900 and 1918 hematite was hauled from the Helen open-pit mine. At this stage the valuable, high-grade iron ore, hematite, gave way to poor-grade siderite. However, with major innovations in production, the mine reopened in 1939 and underground mining operations began, a unique operation for an iron mine because of the high costs involved. The siderite ore was loaded into a sinter furnace, which drives carbon dioxide from the ore thus increasing its iron content sufficiently for the blast furnace. So iron mining continued, both underground and in the open pit.

During all this relentless activity, some adits in the north zone of the MacLeod mine cut through open cavities containing beautiful crystal groups of calcite, quartz, pyrite and marcasite. Even though these minerals are relatively common they occur as such fine display specimens that collectors and museums prize them.

Today the gold prospectors have returned to the Wawa area. A very big strike at Hemlo, barely off the Trans-Canada Highway, has created tremendous excitement and activity. Again men will try to penetrate this tough country the secrets of which Missibize still guards.

Iron, More Valuable than Gold

Iron, which became so important to the support of the Wawa community, is the backbone of our civilization. Although we take iron for granted, the ancient Egyptians valued it more than gold or silver, their only source being those rare meteorites that are largely composed of native iron and nickel. As early as 4000 BC rich and powerful Egyptians coveted lumps of meteoritic iron for their jewellery.

An aggregate of white calcite crystals (3 cm in height) stands amongst dark brown, botryoidal goethite. *J. Schekkerman.*

The MacLeod iron mine as it appeared in
Ontario's wilderness in 1954. *Energy, Mines
and Resources.*

White calcite crystals (1 cm) perched on a crust of bronzy marcasite (iron sulphide), which does not constitute an iron ore because of its low iron content and the associated troublesome sulphur.
J. Schekkerman.

Iron smelting to extract iron metal from very common iron-bearing minerals probably dates back to about 3000 BC. It involved a technological advance over copper and bronze smelting, since heating the ore alone did not render the metal. In addition it had to be hammered to weld droplets of iron together and to squeeze out impurities. The art of iron smelting had developed sufficiently by about 1500 BC to allow a limited trade of manufactured objects and by 800 BC the use of iron for utilitarian articles spread throughout the Old World cultures.

About 2,000 years ago the first simple steel production began: iron was kept hot in the presence of charcoal from which it absorbed carbon; quenching in cold water attained the critical hardening of this carbon steel.

The blast furnace, which produces iron more efficiently, took over in the fourteenth century and the process remains essentially the same today. A mixture of iron ore consisting of iron oxide and silicate impurities, coke, a source of carbon; and limestone burns in the presence of air forced into the base of the furnace. Carbon combining with oxygen from the ore minerals reduces the ore to iron metal. The limestone fuses with ore impurities to form a disposable, slag liquid.

Steel, the major metal of modern industry, is often alloyed with other metals to improve specific physical properties. The elements most commonly added to steels are nickel (for corrosion resistance in stainless steel), chromium (for durability, as in ball bearings), manganese (for hardness, as in gun barrels), tungsten (for hardness and weight, as in armour-piercing shells), molybdenum (for high temperature hardness, as in aircraft wings), vanadium (for resilience, as in car springs) and titanium (for resistance to corrosion and high temperatures, as in rocket parts). Canada, a major producer of nickel, molybdenum and titanium, contributes many of the elements essential to specialized steel alloys.

In spite of Canada's vast mineral wealth, we lack iron ore deposits. This unfortunate anomaly makes the MacLeod mine important to our economy, so it persists in its efforts to keep producing. However, future supplies of this essential metal must now be found.

12
Sudbury: Nickel Capital of the World

Mining
The ore-bearing rock must be of a sufficiency to allow profitable removable of the metal. Miners drill a series of holes into the rock, load them with explosive, and blast. Scrapers or loaders transport the ore to a shaft where it can be hoisted to the surface. *INCO*

". . . I will in like manner explain the principles of under-ground mining . . . so I will describe first of all the digging of shafts, tunnels, and drifts on *venae profundae*;" Text and illustration from *De Re Metallica* (1556), by Georgius Agricola (trans. *Courtesy Dover Publications Inc.*)

Milling

". . . since nature usually creates metals in an impure state, mixed with earth, stones and solidified juices, it is necessary to separate most of these impurities . . . the ores are sorted, broken with hammers, ground into powder, sifted, washed, roasted and calcined." (*De Re Metallica*)

The powdered ore passes through a magnetic separator to remove pyrrhotite. The remainder is processed through a series of flotation tanks. The valuable sulphide minerals float away from the waste silicates by using various chemicals that cause them to adhere to bubbles passing through the solution. Similarly the two sulphides, chalcopyrite and pentlandite, can be separated from each other. *INCO*

Although the presence of copper in the Sudbury region was known as early as 1856, the date celebrated for the discovery of ore there is 1883. During August of that year Thomas Flanagan noticed a rust-coloured patch of rock in an outcrop that had just been blasted for the construction of the Canadian Pacific Railway. News travelled fast and prospectors flocked to the area. They recognized chalcopyrite, a copper iron sulphide, and announced a copper strike.

A great disappointment soon followed the strike. The first ore smelted did not produce pure copper at all, but instead that dreaded "kupfer-nickel". This name, given by the miners of Saxony 200 years ago, refers to the metal they refined from the ore in their minès. Expecting the soft, easy-to-work copper metal, "kupfer", their labour left them instead with a light-coloured, hard metal they could not work. Believing this to be the result of witchcraft they blamed the spell on the devil, or "Old Nick".

Smelting

Chalcopyrite and pentlandite are smelted separately. In a high-temperature furnace the sulphur released from the mineral forms sulphur dioxide. The iron combines with added sand and floats off as slag leaving relatively pure molten copper or nickel metal, which cools and hardens in a cast. In the early years at Sudbury the ore was smelted on huge open wood fires. Extensive felling of timber, required for the hearth, and the noxious sulphur fumes together devastated much of the local landscape. Today, to protect the environment, the companies carefully control the furnace emissions. *INCO.*

''When the ore is smelted, those things which were mixed with the metal before it was melted are driven forth, because the metal is perfected by fire in this manner.''
(*De Re Metallica*)

Refining
"Now I will explain the methods used to separate copper from gold." (*De Re Metallica*)

After smelting a usable metal remains, but often a very pure final product is required. Of several refining processes the most widely used is electrolysis. This consists of dissolving impure metal into solution, then selectively attracting pure metal to a plate by means of an electric current. The impurities resulting from nickel refinement give the useful metal cobalt, while refinement of the remaining residues of copper yields small but significant amounts of gold, silver and platinum. *INCO.*

It was not until 1751 that a Swedish scientist, Axel Cronstedt, successfully separated the kupfer-nickel into its two distinct metals; copper and nickel. Even though the discovery at Sudbury came more than a hundred years later, the separation of nickel remained difficult and its uses limited. The mines faced bankruptcy. Sudbury would then have failed but for the foresight and perseverance of several men in varying occupations: Samuel Ritchie, entrepreneur; Sir John A. Macdonald and Sir Charles Tupper, politicians; Alfred Mond, chemist; John Gamgee, metallurgist; Dr John Thompson, businessman. All believed in the success of Sudbury nickel.

Certainly the Sudbury Basin exhibits one of the most remarkable geological structures in the world. Scientists from every continent have produced almost innumerable studies, theses and arm-waving lectures about the basin, an elliptical area roughly sixty-four by twenty-eight kilometres, and from all this investigation several theories of origin have been produced. One of the more popular ideas is that a huge meteor crashed into the area, creating the basin; the impact caused fractures in the earth's crust that allowed magma to rise from depth. This magmatic intrusion contained significant amounts of nickel and copper.

A 3-mm wide crystal of sperrylite (a platinum arsenide from the Vermilion mine). Canada follows the Republic of South Africa and the USSR in platinum production. The major source is the Sudbury mines. A very rare metal, only a cupful of platinum is recovered for every 30,000 t of ore mined per day. The automotive industry uses half the platinum in North America in catalytic converter exhaust systems. It is also used as a cancer-inhibiting drug, as a catalyst in the manufacture of nitric acid used in fertilizer, and in the production of laser rods, fibreglass and in non-toxic electrical contacts in pacemakers. *J. Schekkerman.*

Extracting Metal from Rock

Man's first metals were those found in their natural state as minerals such as gold, silver and copper. Today most metals require refining from minerals containing several different elements. These compounds do not possess the desirable properties of a metal, and to extract a metal requires a complex series of steps. The most important process, smelting, was developed six thousand years ago.

Even now the processes of obtaining a metal from its parent rock remain complex, though continually evolving with advances in technology. Very simply, the operations involve mining, concentrating the economic minerals and smelting. The Sudbury ore contains approximately 1 per cent each of copper and nickel; except for a very small amount of rare elements the remaining 98 per cent must be removed by the above operations. The most common minerals are pyroxene (calcium-iron-silicate), feldspar (calcium-sodium-aluminum-silicate), olivine (iron-magnesium-silicate), pyrrhotite (iron-sulphide) pentlandite (iron-nickel-sulphide) and chalcopyrite (copper-iron-sulphide).

The initial disappointment of Sudbury has long since passed. Today, as the world's largest single source of nickel, it commands world stature. Nickel, the essential ingredient of stainless steel, finds wide application in both home and industry.

13
Cobalt: the Silver City

Cobalt silver occurred in veins varying in width from a few centimetres to over 2 m. In the early 1900s mining did not require expensive equipment, enabling anyone to seek his fortune. *Cobalt's Northern Ontario Mining Museum*

Headframe of the Colonial mine, located
2 km E of the Cobalt townsite; operating
initially from 1907 to 1937, it produced
38,000 kg of silver. *Doug Robinson.*

Jacques Cartier provided the first written reference to silver in the Cobalt
area. On his second voyage (1535-1536) the Indians signed to him that silver
metal resembling his neck-chain could be found in the ''Kingdom of the
Saguenay''. It lay toward the north, up a great stream (the Ottawa River)
along the mountains (the Laurentians)! Although gold and silver keenly
interested the early explorers, Cartier never made the journey.

Archaeologists have found that during the period from the birth of Christ to about AD 200 natives traded silver throughout an area extending from Ontario south to Georgia and, perhaps, as far as Florida. The LeVesconte burial mound on the Trent River near Campbellford, Southern Ontario, revealed during excavation several pieces of unworked Cobalt ore as well as hammered and rolled sheets of silver. Apparently some silver traded along this eastern corridor remained as a raw material rather than a finished artifact. The Indians fashioned silver into a number of ritualistic, artistic and decorative articles including beads, ear ornaments, buttons and a covering for their musical instrument, the panpipe. These objects, buried with the deceased, indicated his status and wealth. However, for a long time after AD 200 silver slipped from use and, in fact, its next period of utilization came with the Europeans, who presented silver ornaments to prominent Indians, who wore them to express their important position.

The first white man to describe accurately the silver-bearing rocks in the Cobalt area was Monsieur Sieur de Troyes. In his diary dated 24 May 1686 he recounts visiting a "mine" while on his way to oust the English from their trading posts on James Bay. He marked on a map a silver, galena vein on the east shore of Lake Timiskaming some twelve kilometres south of present-day Cobalt. Le Chevalier de Tonty subsequently visited the site but his superiors decided it was too far north of Montreal for profitable exploitation.

Two centuries later a rediscovery of silver in the Timiskaming region took place, credit for which belongs to J.H. McKinley and Ernest Darragh. On 7 August 1903, while scouting for railway ties, the men spotted some gleaming, metallic flakes at the southeast end of Long Lake, later renamed Cobalt Lake. The flakes bent easily and dented between their teeth. They sent samples to Montreal for assaying and the results revealed native silver with an amazingly high concentration of 4,000 ounces to the ton. They filed the claim and there grew the McKinley-Darragh mine.

Some six weeks later, Fred LaRose made his somewhat more celebrated discovery. The story seems unlikely, but because it is such a good tale it has become widely publicized as part of the folklore that distinguishes this community. The stocky smithy, working at his forge one evening, noted a red fox snooping about the camp. Letting fly his hammer he missed the animal but cracked off a piece of rock, exposing the glitter of silver. Irrespective of the means of obtaining the sample, its reality is unquestionable as it yielded the LaRose mine.

The event involved another important character in the history of Cobalt. LaRose's famous silver sample eventually found its way into the hands of Ontario's first provincial geologist, Dr Willet Green Miller, who rushed to visit the site. He arrived in late October and found that four veins had been discovered. Three of these contained large lumps of native silver. Miller returned early in the spring of 1904, as soon as the snow was off the ground. His extensive geological report describing the silver, nickeline and cobalt bloom expressed his enthusiasm for the potential of this mining area. Miller made a second famous contribution to this area, he named the camp Cobalt, in reference to the heavy shiny, cobalt minerals associated with the silver.

Miller's report created absolutely no enthusiasm. Canadians at the time were not willing to take further chances with mining ventures, too many had been stung already. William G. Tretherway, a Cornishman, heard of the strike and headed for Cobalt. Within a week he had two highly successful claims. His first shipment of ore to the south for refining marked the beginning of the prospecting rush. T.W. Gibson described the event in *Mining in Ontario*, ''The shipments consisted of slabs of native metal (silver) stripped off the walls of the vein like boards from a barn.''

Almost overnight prospectors, miners, claim jumpers and promoters flooded into the area. Coleman township became studded with claim posts and the townsite of Cobalt grew out of the bare rock. Certainly no one could foretell that these were the mere beginnings of the great mining industry within the Precambrian Shield. Never destined to boom and bust, Cobalt has had over eighty years of continuous operation with over fifty producing mines totalling 600,420,000 ounces of silver.

By 1905, one year after the mining boom, sixteen mines operated in the area. Production increased to a peak in 1911 when more than thirty-one million ounces of silver were shipped. At this time Cobalt's population tipped the ten thousand mark. The town consisted of tents, boarding-houses and hotels randomly built among the tree stumps. Water had to be carried in pails from the lake, and bathroom facilities consisted of chamber pots and backhouses. Such sanitation facilities bred the largest typhoid epidemic in the history of Ontario. Smallpox and black diphtheria followed. Patients lay in tent hospitals and ''pest houses''; the dead piled up in trenches in the old Farr cemetery. The epidemic lasted from 1906 until 1911 and during this time the only healthy place for the fit was in the bush, far from town.

Wire silver (6 cm long) from the Cobalt Lode mine. Here the silver usually occurred in great sheets and was referred to as "silver pavement". *J. Schekkerman.*

During those early years Cobalt was a boisterous town. It had its cat houses, blind pigs and feuds, but on the whole remained law-abiding. The frenzy associated with tremendous wealth initially kept the fever high. The silver veins close to the surface mined inexpensively, so the possibility of fortune remained for anyone lucky enough to make a big strike. Mines were not large or elaborate like in many other districts in Northern Ontario or Quebec. The community soon settled into one of solidarity and this pride still exists today. Cobalt's history has always been marked by a series of achievements. This was not just one of the largest silver deposits in the world. It had other riches! It boasted one of the finest hockey teams and ladies hard-ball teams in the countryside. Three men skied from Cobalt to Toronto on a single pair of skis six metres long, just to promote their town. Among its ''firsts'' must be recorded the streetcar, which began its service up to New Liskeard in 1910. In the same year the world's only water-powered compressed air plant opened at Ragged Chute to provide the driving force for all the drills, hoists and crushers for all mines in the area. A somewhat lesser engineering feat, but still one of importance, modified a car to make the first snowmobile in the north. Here the Ontario Provincial Police had their beginnings and the events of Cobalt established the laws of The Mining Act; this legislation has become a model followed by other governments throughout the world.

After the First World War, inflation and the miners' strike only dented the economy of Cobalt. The real trouble began on 4 October 1922 with the disastrous Haileybury Fire. Brush burning out of control at Charlton swept south for some sixty kilometres, engulfing the bush and destroying the towns of Charlton, Heaslip, Haileybury and North Cobalt. At Cobalt fate turned the wind and only part of the town burned. For many, the loss of their loved ones, homes or businesses broke them. For those who stayed on to rebuild, the depression of the 1930s lay ahead.

The economic health of Cobalt depends entirely on the condition of the world's metal market. As the depression progressed the demand for silver dropped drastically. Most people anticipated that Cobalt would become a ghost town. Their predictions almost came true but the advent of the Second World War saved the place.

This time it was not silver that saved the town but, strangely enough, the element for which the town was named; cobalt. For a long time minor amounts of cobalt oxide had been required for the famous ''cobalt blue'' in ceramics. Then technology found uses for the metal such as the Cobalt 60 Therapy Unit (the Cobalt Bomb) for cancer treatment and the more mundane but profitable strengthening alloy for steel manufacture of heavy artillery and jet engines — the essentials of war.

The mining of cobalt in conjunction with silver carried the town until 1957. At this time cheaper sources of cobalt were found elsewhere in the world. From then until the present, the Cobalt camp has relied on its silver lining. Surprisingly, the photographic and electronic industries consume most of today's silver production. Any change in these demands could once again jeopardize the existence of this town; but even the casual visitor to this community soon realizes the resilient people here will not let their town die.

14

Bancroft: the Mineral Capital of Canada

Although Bancroft has always been an important lumbering and farming centre, the variety of minerals and the uranium deposits unique to this area have earned this Southern Ontario town world-renown, as the "Mineral Capital of Canada". The Bancroft Gemboree annually attracts thousands of "rockhounds" who come to exhibit, trade and sell minerals and comb the surrounding hills and old mine sites for more treasures. Every major mineral collection in the world proudly exhibits extraordinary specimens of titanite, zircon, hornblende, nepheline and apatite from this area.

A Classic Mineral Locality

For every type of collectable there exist classics: a Rembrandt painting, a Syracuse dekadrachms coin, a Boulle commode. Similarly for minerals certain localities throughout the world become known for fine specimens: wire silver from Kongsberg, Norway; large gold nuggets from California; emeralds from Muzo, Colombia; and serandite crystals from Mont Saint-Hilaire, Quebec. Bancroft, a world classic for giant crystals, has furnished feldspars of up to five metres in width, nephelines of almost two metres, beryls of one metre, hornblendes of over three metres and zircons and titanites of one third of a metre. Crystal growth conditions in these billion-year-old marbles and granites of the Precambrian Shield must have been ideal.

Apatite crystal (length 8 cm) from
Wilberforce. During the later 19th century
this mineral was mined from many pits in
the area providing phosphate for the fertilizer
industry. *J. Schekkerman.*

How large can a crystal grow? A good question with no satisfactory answer. Legend tells of a single feldspar crystal, quarried in the Ural Mountains, that measured 10 metres square and was of unknown length. Regrettably, like most giants, no accurate record exists. The largest authenticated crystal noted of any mineral species describes a beryl from Madagascar, 18 metres in length, 3.5 metres in diameter and weighing approximately three hundred and eighty tonnes. Canada's largest single, recorded crystal, a phlogopite mica from the Lacey mine, Loughborough Township, Ontario, measured over 4 metres in diameter and 10 metres in length, and weighed 330 tonnes.

The existence of giant crystals proclaims nature's patience and excellence in building. Awareness of their rarity will prompt people to record even larger specimens. To pay tribute to this phenomenon, a worthwhile but difficult task would be to collect one of these giants and preserve it from natural erosion or exploitation.

Mineral Uses from Iron to Atomic Energy

Mining in the Bancroft area has been carried out intermittently for over a hundred years, beginning with the Coe Hill iron mine in 1880. Since then the mining history of this area stands out as one of Canada's most diverse. Over a dozen different minerals have been mined for uses extending from Christmas tree "snow" and gemstones to armour plate and atomic bombs.

One of the common rocks in the area contains nepheline and feldspar. Both minerals form important constituents of glass and ceramics as well as bathtub cleaning powders. More recently nepheline has been used in the production of clear plastics.

Sometimes the nepheline rock contains corundum, a mineral second only to diamond in hardness. Mining of corundum in the vicinity peaked during the First World War because it served as a grinding compound in the production of arms. Minor amounts of blue and black sapphire, the coloured gem-variety of corundum, have been found and still keep collectors busily searching.

The latest mining activity around Bancroft has centred on radioactive minerals containing uranium and radium. In 1922 W.W. Richardson found uraninite on the property presently known as the Fission mine and operations from 1929 to 1931 recovered radium. In 1898 the Curies discovered the medical wonder of this element; radiation from radium selectively destroys cancerous tissue. However, radium occurs in uranium minerals to the extent of one part radium to every three million parts of uranium. Not surprisingly, this mining venture ended swiftly due to prohibitively expensive recovery costs. Prior to its closure, an enterprising group bottled water that had seeped into the mine workings and sold it for its "curative powers".

Sodalite from the Princess Sodalite quarry set in a silver box. In 1901 the Duke and Duchess of Cornwall (later King George V and Queen Mary) were presented with a piece of this sodalite; they found it so attractive some was quarried for Marlborough House in London. *J. Schekkerman.*

A cubic crystal of uraninite (1 cm across). This oxide mineral is the most important uranium ore in Canada. *J. Schekkerman.*

In 1939 scientific experimentation uncovered a new source of energy in the nucleus of the uranium atom. The atomic blast that devastated Hiroshima in 1945 marked the advent of nuclear fission. Since that time techniques have been developed to control splitting of atoms in heavily shielded nuclear reactors. The tremendous quantities of heat energy released converts water into steam that drives turbo-generators, which produce electricity. Intermittently from 1947 onward, Bancroft has produced uranium to suit the fluctuating world markets.

Today the Bancroft mines rest quietly, resources still plentiful. The wide variety of minerals there await developments in technology and markets. This potential underlies the spirit of the community like an unplayed card in a poker game, or the yet-to-be discovered mineral classic for the relentless collector.

Uranophane (5-mm spray). Collectors regard the Madawaska mine as a classic locality for this mineral. This calcium-uranium-silicate-hydrate is one of over 70 minerals that contain uranium, but uraninite (uranium-oxide) is the most important ore. Canada possesses almost a third of the known low-cost uranium reserves in the western world. *J. Schekkerman.*

A V-shaped, twinned crystal of titanite
(10 cm long) from Tory Hill. The locality is
world-famous to collectors. *J. Schekkerman.*

The Bancroft area.

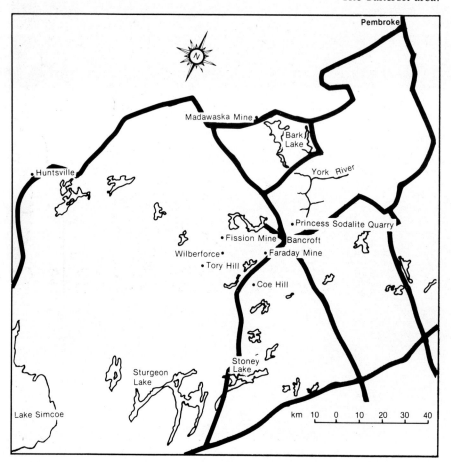

Calcite crystals (7 cm long) coated with goethite. *J. Schekkerman.*

15

Mont Saint-Hilaire, Quebec
Canada's Most Diverse Mineral Locality

Mont Saint-Hilaire rises 400 m above the flat
St Lawrence Lowland. *NMNS*

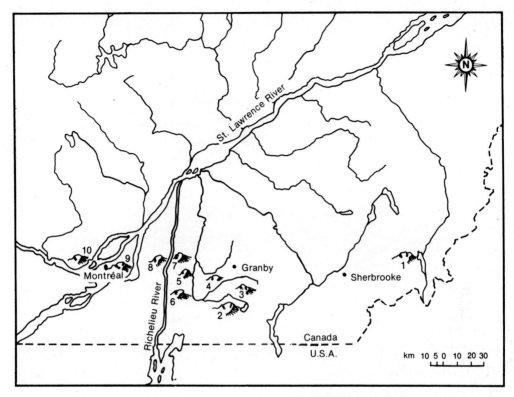

The Monteregian Hills:
1. Megantic; 2. Brome; 3. Shefford;
4. Yamaska; 5. Rougemont; 6. Johnson;
7. Saint-Hilaire; 8. Saint-Bruno; 9. Mount
Royal; 10. Oka.

Brigadier Andrew Hamilton Gault chose an elegant setting for his manor beside Lac Hertel, atop Mont Saint-Hilaire. The surrounding mature trees remain as rare vestiges of the huge forests that covered southwestern Quebec long ago. Upon receiving Gault's bequest in 1958, McGill University divided his estate into a restricted research zone and a public recreational zone. Now anyone can enjoy the woodland paths, the cross-country ski trails and the spectacular view across the Richelieu River towards Mount Saint Bruno and Mount Royal on the far horizon.

Mont Saint-Hilaire, one of ten prominent hills, protrudes above the flat plains of the Saint Lawrence Lowlands. This series of geologically related monadnocks extends for approximately two hundred kilometres. The ten hills from west to east are Oka (30 kilometres west of Montreal), Mount Royal, Saint Bruno, Saint-Hilaire, Johnson, Rougemont, Yamaska, Shefford, Brome and Megantic (50 kilometres east of Sherbrooke). In 1903, Frank Dawson Adams collectively named them the Monteregian Hills, taking the name from Mount Royal (Mons Regius) in Montreal, the best-known member of the group.

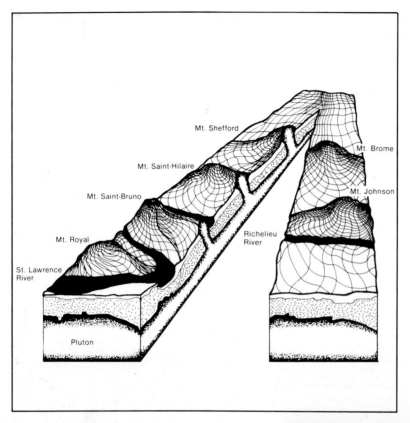

Theoretical profile of the Monteregian Hills showing the relations among the various structures.

Pair of twinned crystals of rhodochrosite (7 mm). *J. Schekkerman.*

Brilliant sample of serandite which makes Mont Saint-Hilaire world-famous; here is a 10 cm crystal with white analcime.
J. Schekkerman.

Geological evidence suggests the Monteregian Hills all derived from the same giant magma chamber, which flowed into overlying rocks along a deep fracture in the earth's crust, now marked by the Saint Lawrence Valley. The portion of these pipes presently exposed would have crystallized approximately three kilometres below the surface a hundred million years ago. Since that time the sedimentary layers of rock above the intrusions have gradually eroded due to eons of relentless weather and grinding ice, leaving the resistant, harder magmatic rocks as a series of circular mounds. Mont Saint-Hilaire measures almost four kilometres in diameter and rises four hundred metres above the valley floor.

**Example of a hexagonal crystal of catapleiite,
a rare mineral much sought after by
collectors.** *J. Schekkerman.*

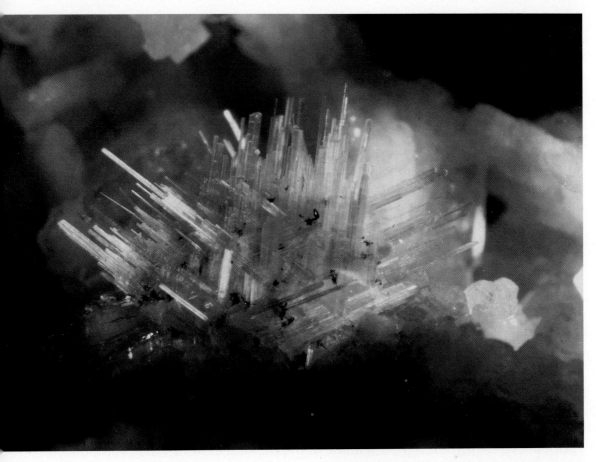

Example of the phenomena that collectors of micro-minerals can observe: the growth of a reticulated crystal of epididymite (3.5 cm). *J. Schekkerman.*

In addition to the recreational facilities there have been some economic incentives: associated with the Monteregian plutons exist intrusions known as kimberlites. These rocks originate deep in the earth's crust and those found in South Africa, Siberia and Arkansas contain diamonds. Spurred on by this knowledge men, longing to find another source of the world's most coveted gem, have crushed and searched tonnes of rock, unfortunately to no avail. More mundane but still important, syenite rock quarried at Mont Saint-Hilaire constitutes the major portion of a special concrete used in construction.

Mineral Collecting as a Hobby

Mineral collecting usually attracts the individual keenly interested in details that constitute the order and beauty of nature. Each lowly insect, intricate flower and perfect crystal has its place and significance. Plants and animals exist as fragile transients on a very thin shell, or biosphere, over the massive, persistent rocks.

For the novice the initial problem lies in *choosing a site*. In Canada one does not lack opportunity: outings may range from dodging grissly bears and scaling cliffs in the Kluane Mountains to taking a bus to the local quarry outside Hamilton. Limitations depend only on time, distance and the rest of the family's patience. A guidebook helps the choice, but why not be venturesome and find a new outcrop or road cut? This hobby thrives on innovation and it guarantees success to those who look long and close enough. Do not forget the fringe benefits of fresh air and exercise!

Tools should be simple and inexpensive: safety glasses, one-handed crack hammer, rock chisel, carry-bag and papers for wrapping specimens. With experience many specialized tools could be added: pry bars, sledges, rock drills and wedges. An excess of equipment will only make you wish you collected moths rather than minerals.

A *mineral collection* eventually has limits, usually defined by space or weight. For these reasons, collectors often specialize by locality, species or specimen size. A collection's most important feature, the catalogue, records the number attached to each specimen and its corresponding detailed locality information. Oddly enough, the name of the mineral assumes minor importance as it can be added to the notes at any time. For those with limited experience, identification usually follows consultation with books, fellow collectors or professionals. Mineral collecting should always be fun; remember to show respect for safety and for the property being visited.

Crystal of vesuvianite (6 mm.) *J. Schekkerman.*

Mineral Collecting at Mont Saint-Hilaire

In the early 1960s the wealth of mineral specimens at Mont Saint-Hilaire became known. During operations at the Poudrette and Demix quarries, cavities containing fascinating crystals were exposed. Shortly afterwards scientific articles written by various Canadian authors appeared in the journals. Spectacular prismatic crystals of orange serandite measuring as much as thirteen centimetres in length were first to attract attention. Well-formed rhombs of siderite up to twenty-five centimetres filled large vugs. Clear, colourless, hexagonal plates of the very rare mineral, catapleiite, certainly rate highly with collectors. Single, white crystals of analcime, as large as a dinner plate, have been collected. Yet many of the most beautiful and spectacular finds require magnification.

Micro-mounts, as they are termed, form a separate section of mineral collecting. A whole new world of perfect crystals unfolds with the aid of a microscope; shiny black pyramidal crystals of brookite, dark green needles of acmite, cruciform steacyite, dodecahedra of bright blue sodalite and colourless snowflakes of epididymite.

Appendix 3 lists 180 minerals known to occur at Saint-Hilaire. The geology, mineralogy and chemistry of the locality is so complex that a number of collectors and investigators have devoted most of their efforts to its study. They have formed their own club and publish a regular newsletter entitled *The St. Hilaire News*.

This famous site has attracted people from around the world in such numbers that the quarry owners restrict entrance to special groups on specific days. Few localities anywhere can surpass the expectations of Mont Saint-Hilaire.

16
A Mineral Locality in Montreal City

The Francon quarry, on Montreal Island, provides an excellent example of a famous mineral site located within city limits. Limestone, quarried for cement and road material, contains little of interest for mineral collectors. But this operation exposed a sill of rock with exotic and rare minerals: no less than sixty different minerals have been identified including six species new to the science of mineralogy.

A sill describes a flat-lying sheet of rock intruded between sedimentary beds. In the quarry walls of Francon the sill appears as a light-coloured band of rock in the grey limestone layers. In contrast, dikes, more readily evident than sills, cut across the beds of rock they intrude. The Francon sill magma, derived from a large chamber of molten rock, seems to be part of the Monteregian Hills intrusion described in the previous chapter.

Triboluminescence: Energy at Odds
Light visible to our eyes derives from two sources: incandescence, where material heated to a sufficiently high temperature (over 550° Celsius) radiates light energy, like the sun, incandescent light bulbs and "red hot" metal; and luminescence, where the material absorbs one form of energy, then re-emits it as visible light.

The various types of luminescence receive names according to the incident energy source. Photoluminescence describes the glow of road signs from a car's headlamps; bioluminescence describes a biochemical process such as in a firefly's glow; and cathodluminescence in television results from an electron beam impinging on a fluorescent screen.

**The sill containing the rare minerals is the
distinct layer situated about a third of the
depth of the Francon quarry.** *Geological
Survey of Canada.*

Triboluminescence, a phenomenon of nature unfamiliar to many, defines light energy produced by pressure. This conversion of energy forms, though not well understood, is exemplified in a few minerals such as quartz, some samples of fluorite and mica, and weloganite, a mineral unique to the Francon quarry. The crushing of a crystal of weloganite causes it to glow a faint blue. This is not like a spark produced by striking flint and steel.

Spheres of fine radiating fibres of dresserite,
each approximately 1 mm in diameter.
J. Schekkerman.

The physical structure of the atom is best understood in the early concepts of Bohr (1913). He describes a central core of hard spheres consisting of protons and neutrons surrounded by a cloud of electrons. The electrons orbit in concentric shells outside the nucleus, much as planets orbit about a sun. For an atom in its normal state the electrons orbit in consistent and well defined paths, but when the atom experiences an addition of energy it becomes excited: electrons jump into shells further from the nucleus, almost immediately falling back to their normal orbit; this relaxation produces light energy.

Weloganite is named in honour of W.E. Logan, first Director of the Geological Survey of Canada and the National Museums of Canada. These crystals measure 1.5 cm in length. *J. Schekkerman.*

Beautiful acicular groups of dawsonite crystals (8 mm across). *J. Schekkerman.*

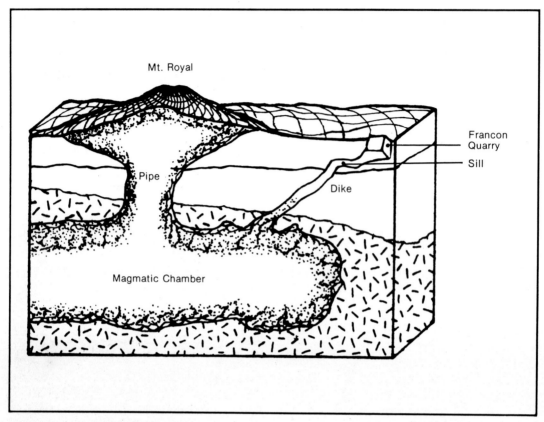

Idealized section showing possible
relationship of the Francon sill to Mount
Royal.

   The grinding of weloganite produces the energy transfers described
above, resulting in the light energy of triboluminescence. The actual mechan-
ism by which pressure causes electrons to move into a higher energy orbital
is not understood and remains a problem requiring fundamental research.
   Although newspapers and television highlight expeditions to the wilderness of the far north in search of new mineral finds, one should never forget
to look in the backyard as well. There always exists that thrill of finding
something where you least expect it, as in the case of the rare minerals of
the Francon quarry: a reminder that ''gold is where you find it''.

Jeffrey mine, Asbestos, Quebec. As much as
40,000,000 t of rock and ore is removed
annually from this pit, which is 1,250 m wide
and 275 m deep. *Geological Survey of Canada*.

17

The Jeffrey Mine, Asbestos, Quebec
The Western World's Largest Asbestos Deposit

This grossular crystal measures 1 cm across, but crystals 3 times this size have been found. The trapezohedral face is striated due to oscillatory growth between this form and the dodecahedral form. *J. Schekkerman.*

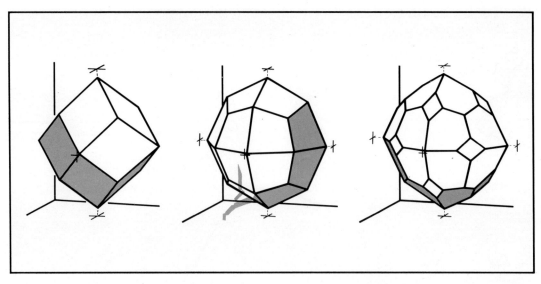

The garnet crystal structure is in the cubic crystal system, hence crystal forms are equidimensional. The most common forms are the 12-sided dodecahedron (left) and the 24-sided trapezohedron (middle). Many of the grossular crystals found in the Jeffrey mine are combinations of these two forms (right), with shiny dodecahedral faces and striated trapezohedral faces.

Eighteenth-century reports of the remote eastern townships of southern Quebec indicate that both the Indians of the area and early settlers knew of asbestos fibre. For warmth Indians stuffed the peculiar woolly mineral into their moccasins and farmers' wives collected asbestos from outcrops and from ploughed-up rocks to knit socks and mittens.

Not until 1881 (some five years after the discovery of the nearby Thetford mines asbestos deposit) did Evan Williams, a visiting Welsh slate miner, recognize the potential of the chrysotile occurrence, a local curiosity on the property of Charles Webb. Williams persuaded W.H. Jeffrey to open a mine, which operated on a royalty basis, paying the farm owner $10 for a tonne of fibre in the summer and $5 a tonne in the winter. Today the Jeffrey mine operates in the second largest (after Asbest in the USSR) asbestos deposit in the world. This open pit alone produces about 13 per cent of the world's chrysotile asbestos, amounting to some six hundred thousand tonnes a year.

Fibres of chrysotile, 2 cm long, are the main
asbestos ore. *J. Schekkerman.*

Abestos: the "Immortal Linen"

Asbestos derives from the Greek, *asbestus*, meaning incombustible. The
description comes from Pliny (AD 23 to AD 73), who refers to a rare cloth,
linum vivum (immortal linen), which the Romans wove into a cremation
shroud for their kings. Accounts of even earlier uses date back to at least
2500 BC, when the inhabitants of the Lake Juojarvi region of east Finland
strengthened their earthenware pots and cooking utensils with an asbestos
mineral.

Today the term asbestos defines the physical size of fibres which come
from several different minerals, varying widely in chemical composition.
Anthophyllite, ferrogedrite (amosite variety), tremolite, actinolite and rie-
beckite (crocidolite variety) members of the amphibole group and chrysotile, a member of the serpentine group, comprise the principal "asbestos
minerals". Chrysotile, a hydrated magnesium silicate, is by far the most
commercially valuable.

Diopside crystal (2 cm long) on orange grossular. *J. Schekkerman.*

Pectolite bundles measuring 6 mm. Fibres can
be needle-like, causing a good deal of pain to
the unwary collector. *J. Schekkerman.*

The uses of asbestos depend on the mineral's strength, heat and chemical resistance, flexibility, fibre length and incombustibility. A few of the products include reinforced cement building materials, insulation in home appliances and rockets, brake linings, wrapping paper and filters.

Unfortunately the physical properties that make asbestos useful also make it a carcinogen. Fibres, capable of piercing lung tissue, promote cancerous growth. Crysotile accounts for 95 per cent of today's asbestos market and comforting experimental evidence demonstrates it as the least harmful fibre. Even though the present asbestos dust levels in our cities, and even in the asbestos mines, remain insufficient to cause a health risk, society must decide what constitutes an acceptable environmental hazard, keeping in mind that any asbestos substitute may create different medical problems or be less effective in, for example, fire protection or brake linings.

Hessonite Grossular: "Cinnamon Stone"

The Jeffrey mine is world famous not only for its vast asbestos reserves but also for its exceptional crystals of grossular, diopside and vesuvianite. These three minerals comprise a rare rock type associated with serpentine formation and named rodingite after the Roding River, New Zealand, where it was first found and described.

Grossular garnet, as pure calcium aluminum silicate, appears colourless or white, but with the addition of minor amounts of metal ions in the crystal structure it becomes coloured. Iron induces shades of pink and orange while chromium gives a beautiful green hue. All of these varieties of grossular have been found in the Jeffrey mine but certainly orange-coloured hessonite or "cinnamon stone" remains the most popular. Since 1950, perhaps even earlier, specimens of hessonite have been widely distributed throughout North America and Europe. This stone may be cut into beautiful gems because of its hardness and brilliance. In the National Museum of Natural Sciences the largest cut hessonite weighs 24 carats, which probably marks the largest facetted stone from this locality.

Rhombic prehnite (1 cm across) on pink
grossular. *J. Schekkerman.*

The contrast between the beautiful, rare, frivolous, gemmy grossular
and the drab, common, useful chrysotile asbestos has become even more
marked today. These two geologically associated minerals can be likened
to the beauty and the beast. The environmental and related political problems
of asbestos products have reduced the Jeffrey mine to one-tenth of its former
activity. This situation emphasizes the fragile economic nature of a mineral
deposit: supply, mining costs, market uses, environmental hazards and political involvement all determine a mine's viability. Since Canada remains the
world's potentially largest asbestos exporter, the present lull significantly
harms our economy.

A tetragonal crystal of apophyllite, 3 cm
long. *J. Schekkerman.*

18
Lapis Lazuli from Baffin Island

Looking from Glencoe Island towards the
rugged coastline of Baffin Island. Glencoe has
always provided a good campsite for Inuit
seal hunters in this part of the Hudson
Strait. *NMNS*.

Lapis lazuli from Baffin Island can be cut into cabochons. The largest shown is 2 cm.
J. Schekkerman.

Lapis Lazuli: the Gemstone of Pharaohs

The mere mention of the beautiful blue gem lapis lazuli brings to mind the royal treasures found in the ancient tombs of Ur and Egypt. Some superb pieces of jewellery worn by Princess Sit Har-Hor Yunet of the Twelfth Dynasty (*c.* 1700 BC) include turquoise, carnelian and lapis lazuli inlaid in gold. Artisans worked the same gems with leaf gold for the funerary mask of King Tutankhamun (*c.* 1350 BC).

Later in the Bronze Age lapis lazuli began to be used as a pigment. The name comes from an ancient Persian word *lazhward* meaning blue and the Greek word *lapis* meaning stone. When powdered it yields an intense blue pigment known as ultramarine.

Usually three minerals comprise the rock known as lapis lazuli: blue grains of lazurite mottled by white calcite and flecked with inclusions of brass-yellow pyrite. The finest gem lapis has a deep, even, blue colour with no white patches. Unfortunately for the consumer, cut stones have often been touched up with dye to colour the white areas. To further confuse the buyer, imitations such as glass or blue-dyed chalcedony (a variety of quartz) commonly fill the shops. The latter, referred to as Swiss lapis or German lapis, one detects with less difficulty than the synthetic lapis manufactured by Pierre Gilson of Paris, which contains actual inclusions of pyrite.

Baffin Island: a Formidable Land

> Who so maketh Navigations to these countries, hath not only extreme winds, and furious Seas, to encounter withall, but also many monstrous and great Islands of ice: a thing both rare, wonderful and greatly to be regarded.

Dionyse Settle (1577)

The earliest written reports about Baffin Island come from the logs of explorers seeking the northwest passage to the Orient. Sir Martin Frobisher convinced English financiers of the existence of such a route to the north of North America. He returned from his first voyage in 1576 with samples of worthless "gold ore" but his promoter, with the help of a false assay, raised sufficient funds for a second voyage. Queen Elizabeth I supplied the venturer with a ship in which he hauled back two hundred tonnes of ore from Frobisher Bay. A third expedition soon set out, to return with even more rock from mines around Kodlunarn Island in the Countess of Warwick Sound; when it proved devoid of gold they never returned.

Little interest was shown in the geology of this southern area of Baffin Island until early in this century when the Hudson Bay Company trenched a number of prospects for mica. They shipped it to England for stove windows and electrical insulators.

The name spinel, from the Latin ''spinella''
meaning little thorn, is probably in allusion
to the spine-shaped octahedral crystal. This
crystal, found near Lake Harbour, measures
1 cm. *J. Schekkerman.*

The lapis lazuli deposit of southern Baffin Island lies fifteen kilometres north of Lake Harbour, a settlement famous for its Inuit carvers. The "blue rock" has been known by the Inuit for decades but did not appear in any reports until the detailed geological mapping of the area in 1959. It lies within a marble that forms part of a series of highly metamorphosed sedimentary rocks. The original sediments, probably deposited in a restricted marine environment, formed an evaporite.

The Egyptians quarried the earliest known locality for lapis lazuli in the Badakhshan province of Afghanistan. In addition to this area the most important deposits today lie in the Bystroya River valley, Siberia and in the Chilean Andes. The Baffin Island lapis, presently under claim with local Inuit, has not been developed. Due to the unstable political environment of the present world sources, this deposit may warrant further investigation in the future.

Other Gems in the Marble of Southern Baffin Island

Associated with the lapis deposit is a member of the feldspar group called oligoclase. Although feldspar constitutes the most common mineral of the earth's surface this particular occurrence deserves mention. Large crystals, with faces of up to forty centimetres in width, have developed here. Cleavable masses of the mineral range from transparent to translucent and shade from white to pale blue in colour. The material can be cut into beautiful cabochons or, in rare cases, superb facetted gems of up to seven carats. One of the most striking features of this oligoclase, the even striped pattern, results from twinning during crystal growth. For this particular type of twin, two crystals of oligoclase relate to each other by a mirror image. During crystallization the crystal structure periodically reverses itself, giving a lamellar pattern. Some minerals, such as feldspar, commonly have twin growths; because it requires little or no extra energy to grow in one orientation or the other, they oscillate. In the marbles of southern Baffin Island there occur a number of other exotic and rare minerals such as clinohumite, scapolite, titanite and, of particular interest to collectors, fine crystals of spinel. The well formed octahedral crystals are dark blue to purple. Spinel has historical significance both as the stone set prominently in front of the Imperial State Crown of England and as the stone on top of the crown of the Empress Catherine II of Russia. These red-coloured spinels were probably mistakenly identified as ruby, the red-coloured variety of corundum.

This oligoclase feldspar has a striped appearance due to twinning of the crystal structure. Specimen is 12 cm long. The facetted oligoclase gem weighs 7 carats. *J. Schekkerman.*

Although lapis lazuli remains the focal point of interest in the area, any development of the deposit may reveal other, less celebrated, but certainly beautiful, gems. Imagine the excitement of a set of jewels from the far north including ice-blue oligoclase, emerald-green diopside, royal-purple spinel and honey-brown hornblende. However, it would be necessary to replace the mineral names with gem names in order to protect the buyer's vanity.

19
Labradorite "Fire Rock" from Nain, Labrador

Labradorite, Canada's first-described and most celebrated gemstone, flashes with the blues, greens, golds and reds that the Indians described as "fire". This calcium-rich feldspar appears almost black, displaying its brilliant colours only when caught in light from a specific direction. Although the earth's crust contains a lot of feldspar, one rarely finds this particular species of the group. Labradorite no longer comes just from Labrador; other notable localities have now been discovered in Oregon, Finland and Madagascar.

The iridescent colour-flashes of labradorite result from the diffraction of light through thin layers, much like the rainbows observed in soap bubbles or in oil slicks on water. Alternating thicknesses of atomic layers act as the diffraction grating. The colour visible in labradorite depends on the thicknesses of these submicroscopic layers. Red diffracts from slightly thicker layers than blue, and minor changes in the mineral's chemistry determine these thicknesses.

Labrador: Earth's Primaeval Land
Nine thousand years of history:
Three and one-half billion years of time.

The northern coast of Labrador near Saglek Bay boasts a portion of some of the oldest rocks known on earth.

At one time it was joined to Greenland, where matching geology occurs and where ancient sediments and volcanics formed the same land mass, which has been age dated at 3.6 billion years. Since molten planet Earth had its fiery beginning approximately five billion years ago, they stand as almost the earliest part of the earth's solid crust that still remains.

Nain, looking from Ship Hill across Kauk
Harbour towards Paul Island; the dark, worn
rocks that contain the feldspar labradorite are
visible. *NMNS*.

The iridescent colours of this labradorite
specimen (9 cm across) make it suitable for
cutting into fine jewellery stones.
J. Schekkerman.

Following the retreat of the Laurentide glacier, ten thousand years ago, the Maritime Archaic people moved into this land. A nine-thousand-year-old burial site of an Indian boy at L'anse Amour, Strait of Belle Isle, marks the earliest known record of these inhabitants. Not for another eight thousand years (AD 986) did Europeans sight the coast of Labrador. The historic Viking tales of Bjarni Herjolfssom include the first descriptions of North America. Later, Leif Eiriksson and others frequented the coast to collect timber.

The exact landfall of John Cabot in 1497 remains speculative but his discoveries laid English claim to the lands of Labrador and Newfoundland. The Portuguese soon followed, naming the land *Terra del Labrador* in recognition of Juan Fernandez, Don Labrador, who sighted this land in 1501. The coast of Labrador attracted English, Portuguese, French and Spanish fishermen and traders as well as explorers looking for the elusive North West Passage, but it was not until the 1770s that Moravian missionaries established the first permanent European settlement.

Nain, Labrador

"C'est la terre que Dieu donne à Cayn"

Jacques Cartier (1534).

Nain, established in 1771, became the earliest European settlement on the north coast of Labrador and today it remains the northernmost permanent community in the province. This part of Labrador marks the most northerly extent of the treeline. The valleys support small black spruce and the occasional stand of tamarack, but the vegetation consists largely of grasses, mosses and lichens. Hills of dark, rugged, barren rock dominate the landscape, creating a severe and sombre atmosphere. The rough coast-line, broken by deep inlets and dotted with hundreds of islands, stretches on in a navigational maze.

Along this coastline early Moravian missionaries spotted the iridescence of labradorite. Reverend B. Latrobe first describes the mineral as "occurring not only in pebbles on the shore but in spots in the rocks in the neighbourhood of Nain and particularly near a lagoon, about 50 or 60 miles inland, in which Nain north river terminates. Its colours darting through the limpid crystal of the lake, and flashing from the cliffs more especially when moistened by a shower of rain, changing continually with every alteration in the position of the boat, are described as almost realizing a scene in fairy land".

This discovery and the subsequent scientific mineralogical description of this mineral in the late 1700s, by Cronstedt in Sweden, probably establishes the first new mineral from Canada ever to be described. Early textbooks give Paul Island as the type locality for the original mineral description, but there exist several sites from which labradorite can be collected. The larger crystals, of up to several centimetres, displaying good flashes of colour are used for jewellery. Rings, pendants, necklaces and bracelets wrought from this semiprecious gemstone distinguish themselves elegantly. Unfortunately, very little of this jewellery is available, not because of the mineral's rarity around Nain but because of a lack of concerted effort to develop the quarries in this severe and remote area. Attempts at mining gem material on Tabor Island ceased approximately two decades ago.

A second use of labradorite has barely been explored. Many readers may have noted dark-coloured building stones with blue flashes in the sunlight. This rock, similar to that found in Labrador, usually comes from Norway. Enormous quantities of this labradorite building stone exist on the islands and mainland over Nain, but to date only one building in Toronto, on Eglinton Avenue, has been faced with it. Potential exists for large-scale quarrying of this beautiful decorative stone, useful for building facing, monuments, floor tiles and table and counter tops.

20
Ancient Lavas
Bay of Fundy, Nova Scotia

Cape Split juts into the Bay of Fundy at the N extent of the North Mountain basalt. This portion displays spectacularly the earliest and thickest of the lava flows. *Sherman Hines, Masterfile.*

Some two hundred million years ago, during the Triassic period, a long series of tension gashes opened up along what is now the eastern margin of the North American Continent. These deep-reaching channels allowed molten rock to rise, intruding the existing rock as dikes and sills and in some areas pouring out onto the surface as lava flows. These flows can be found sporadically all the way from the Bay of Fundy to North Carolina.

Fissure lava flows cannot be thought of as the classic volcanoes typified by Vesuvius or Mount Saint Helens, cones which spew forth lava or ash; such volcanoes, although spectacular, would appear negligible when compared to the Triassic flood basalts. Here, fissures or volcanic vents extending for many kilometres opened and a highly fluid lava poured out in enormous quantities. A single flow might have been metres thick and have covered several thousand square kilometres.

When basaltic lava reaches the surface of the earth it chills quickly, immediately forming a crust. The resulting igneous rock consists mainly of dark-coloured glass and a fine-grained mass of plagioclase feldspar and pyroxene crystals. Large amounts of water and other volatiles keep these lavas fluid on their ascent to the surface. Once free of the confining pressure of surrounding rock the gases bubble off creating centimetric oval or spherical cavities, called vesicles, in the upper portions of the plastic lava. Water separating from the congealing lava concentrates a number of soluble ions, notably calcium, sodium, potassium, silicon and aluminum, which combine to form low-temperature minerals such as quartz and members of the zeolite group. These late minerals crystallize in the vesicles or fractures of the basalt.

The Bay of Fundy, originally a basin above sea level, experienced four or five flows, the first flow being half the total thickness, which measures approximately two hundred metres. Today the basin, covering an area of about thirty thousand square kilometres, is largely submerged with only small areas exposed along the north coast of the Bay of Fundy: at Grand Manan Island, Isle Haute, Cape d'Or and Five Islands and on the south shore along the North Mountain ridge (which measures approximately seven kilometres in width and extends for two hundred kilometres from Cape Split to Brier Island in the southwest). Since their emplacement the flows have remained relatively undisturbed with only a slight tilting of a few degrees to the northwest and minor local faulting.

Agate, a fine-grained, colour-banded variety
of quartz, occurs as a fracture filling in the
area's oldest lava flow at Economy Mountain,
Amethyst Cove, Cape Blomidon and Scots
Bay. Nova Scotia agates rival any in the
world for colour and interesting patterns,
making them excellent stones for jewellery.
Specimen is 5 cm wide. *J. Schekkerman.*

Close observation reveals the beauty and symmetry of this spray of natrolite crystals. Each prismatic crystal is approximately 1 cm long. *J. Schekkerman.*

Zeolite: the Stone that Boils

Zeolites from the North Mountain cliffs comprise a small number of a large group of minerals with over forty species, all having structural and chemical similarities. In 1756 Freiherr Axel Fredrick Cronstedt, a Swedish mineralogist, submitted a number of crystals to the heat of a blowpipe for chemical testing and noted their peculiar frothing characteristics. He named these minerals, zeolites, from the Greek word for boiling stones.

This fascinating boiling feature of zeolites results from their unique, porous crystal structure. Unlike other crystal structures, the framework has cages or holes large enough to accommodate ions of calcium, sodium and potassium or a molecule of water. The zeolitic-water may be easily driven off with a little heat. In fact some zeolites dehydrate at room temperature in a low relative humidity. This leaves voids in the crystal structure, which lead to some important uses for these minerals.

Another feature of the zeolite structure, important in differentiating species, is how the basic building blocks of the structure join together. These building blocks consist of a silicon or aluminum atom bonded to four oxygen atoms in a tetrahedral configuration. If tetrahedra link in one direction, forming chains, the zeolite has a fibrous habit; such as mesolite, natrolite and scolecite. Strong linkages in two directions result in a planar structure and crystals of this type tend to be platy; such as heulandite and stilbite. The last possibility, equal linkage in all three directions, gives a three-dimensional framework structure which results in equant crystals like analcime, chabazite and mordenite. Although the habit, or crystal form, may give some indication of the species of zeolite it usually requires specialized equipment to obtain a precise identification.

Heulandite and stilbite may be found in vesicles and fractures in any exposure of zeolites in the lavas of Nova Scotia. Both minerals are white, but often stilbite tends to be coloured in shades of yellow, orange and brown. These platy minerals so resemble each other it requires close scrutiny to differentiate the lozenge-shaped outline of heulandite and the double-edged sword form of stilbite.

This large cavity (10 cm) in the basalt contains two zeolite minerals: orange chabazite and white analcime. *J. Schekkerman.*

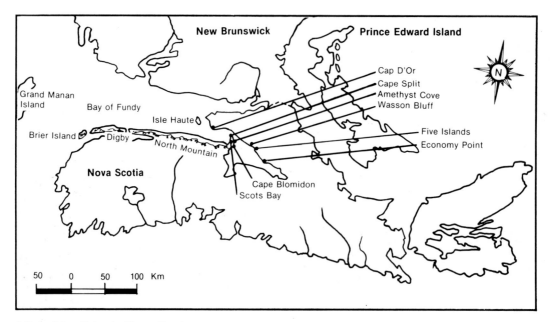

Mineral localities in Nova Scotia.

Since first described in 1829, chabazite specimens from Wasson's Bluff have been circulated to museum collections around the world and hence have become the most famous of Nova Scotia's zeolites. Chabazite, though usually white, in this area ranges in colour from orange to salmon; a uniqueness that earned it the variety, or descriptive, name "acadialite", coined in 1830 and only recently dropped from usage. Acadialite honours the Acadians who lived in this area until the mid eighteenth century, when the British loaded them onto ships at a harbour near Grand Pré and deposited them at several ports along the coastline. This historic site inspired Longfellow's love poem, "Evangeline", which portrays a ficticious incident during this injustice.

This stilbite (3 cm) resembles a sheaf of
wheat, hence its old name, desmine, from
the Greek *desme*, meaning bundle.
J. Schekkerman.

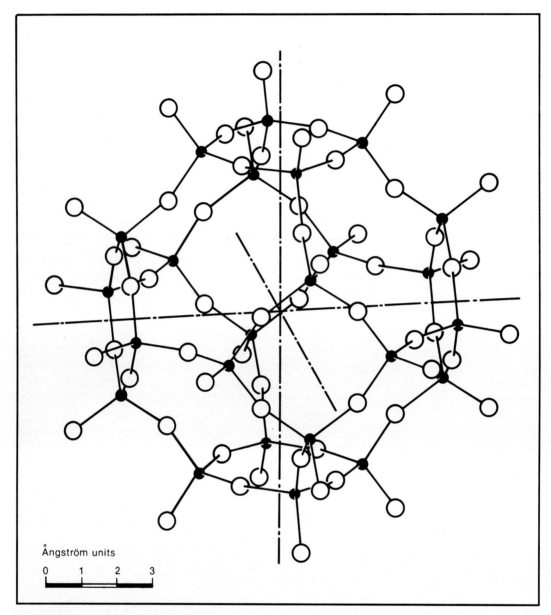

Ångström units

0   1   2   3

Fundamental to all zeolite crystal structures is
a framework built up by silicon and
aluminum atoms (black) surrounded by
4 oxygen (white) atoms. These linked
tetrahedra form cage-like structures, with
some voids measuring several angstroms.
A large atom measures approximately
1 angstrom (1/100,000,000 cm).

In 1925 Chabazite became the first zeolite used in adsorption studies. Observation showed that dehydrated crystals would retain or adsorb small organic molecules and reject larger ones. This phenomenon, described as "molecular sieving", instigated a new industry. Nowadays a large number of different natural and synthetic zeolites are used for the following: removal of radioactive elements from low-level waste streams of nuclear installations; treatment of sewage by removing toxic ammonia compounds that kill fish and promote algae growth; pollution control as an adsorbent in oil-spill cleanup; purification of sour natural gas or gas produced from sewage and decaying garbage; energy production through the incorporation of zeolites as "boosters" in solar panels or heat reservoirs; blood purification in dialysis machines; and for household water softening in the ion exchanger tank.

Several countries including the United States, Japan, Italy and Hungary mine natural deposits of zeolites to support the rising demand for these minerals. Canada has not explored her occurrences in Nova Scotia or central British Columbia but this may be essential soon, due to the expense of manufacturing synthetics. Who knows but what was originally observed as a local curiosity along the Fundy coast may one day lead to a new mining industry for Canada.

Appendix 1
Glossary of Technical Terms

Acicular. Needle shaped.

Adit. Horizontal or inclined passageway that enters a mine from the surface.

Aggregate. Collection of grains or substances united into a mass.

Bloom. Ore decomposed by surface oxidation.

Botryoidal. Rounded masses resembling a bunch of grapes.

Breccia. Angular fragments of rock that have been cemented together by a finer-grained matrix.

Cabochon. Stone cut and polished for ornamental use. Often the grinding is done by hand resulting in a smooth dome shape as opposed to a facetted gem.

Carat. Measure of weight equivalent to one fifth of a gram.

Cleavage. Tendency for a mineral to split along a planar surface.

Crystal. Regular, repeating arrangement of atoms, which often display symmetric planar faces.

Cubo-octahedral. Forms cube and octahedron.

Dodecahedron, dodecahedral. Crystal form in the cubic system having twelve equivalent faces, usually rhombic or diamond shaped.

Drusy. Crust or aggregate of small crystals.

Element. Simple substance composed of identical atoms, e.g. silver, oxygen, calcium.

Escarpment (or scarp). Abrupt rise in land, often a cliff, which extends a long distance across the countryside.

Facet. Flat surface ground and polished on a gemstone to give it brilliance. The technique used involves machinery that can hold the stone to give the correct angles and sizes for each plane.

Fissure. Crack in a rock that has opened. The separation may remain empty or fill with other minerals (*cf.* **fracture**).

Form. All faces on a crystal that are related by symmetry.

Fracture. Break in a rock whether it has remained closed or not. (*cf.* **fissure**).

Granite. Coarse grained, magmatic rock that formed deep within the earth's crust and in some cases intruded rocks above it. It consists primarily of the minerals quartz, feldspar and mica.

Headframe. Housing for the hoisting of equipment that carries men and rock from deep in a mine to the surface.

Intrusion, intrude. Magmatic rock that intrudes pre-existing rock.

Kilogram. Weight of 1 000 grams approximately equalling 2.2 pounds.

Kilometre. Length of 1 000 metres approximately equalling 1,093 yards.

Lamellar. Parallel arrangement of platy crystals.

Lode deposit. Zone of economically desirable minerals within consolidated rock.

Magma. Molten rock usually derived from deep in the earth and capable of intrusion (like a granite) or extrusion as a lava.

Marble. Metamorphic rock composed of calcite or dolomite.

Melt. Liquid state of a substance of the same chemical composition, e.g. water — ice.

Metamorphic. Changes in crystallinity or mineralogy through increases in temperature and/or pressure and/or chemical composition.

Mineral. Naturally occurring substance having a definite chemical composition and usually with an ordered arrangement of atoms.

Monadnock.   Hill of erosion-resistant rock that rises conspicuously above a surrounding plain.

Mucking.   Removal of waste material loosened in a mine-blasting operation.

Native element.   Chemical element that exists as a mineral, i.e. naturally occurring gold, silver and iron.

Nodule.   Rounded body.

Octahedron, octahedral.   Crystal form in the cubic system having eight equivalent triangular faces.

Oscillatory growth.   Repeated parallel growth of crystals having slightly different orientations.

Outcrop.   The portion of rock exposed on the earth's surface.

Pluton.   Magmatic intrusion that emplaces deep in the earth's crust, never erupting at the surface.

Prismatic crystal.   Crystal form defined by three or more planes whose intersections are parallel lines.

Pseudomorph.   When one mineral replaces another mineral and retains the predecessor's form.

Pyramidal terminations.   Group of crystal faces, usually three, four or six, coming to a point.

Rhombs, rhombohedral.   Crystal form in which each of six faces has an identical parallelogram and they are all symmetrically related.

Rock.   Solid, naturally occurring compound generally consisting of more than one mineral.

Scalenohedron, scalenohedral.   Crystal form in the tetragonal or hexagonal crystal systems having faces that are equivalent, scalene triangles.

Scarp, *see* **Escarpment.**

Schiller.   Lustre or iridescence due to internal reflection in a mineral.

Sediment.   Particles of rock or mineral that originate from weathering and erosion and are subsequently transported and deposited.

Sintering.   Melting an ore and removing the silica-rich liquid.

Smelting.   To melt a rock and selectively extract the desired metals.

Suite of rocks.   Rocks occurring together in the same geological environment.

Trapezohedron, trapezohedral.   Crystal form in the cubic system having twenty-four equivalent, kite-shaped faces.

Twin.   Symmetrical intergrowth of two or more crystals of the same mineral species.

Vesicles.   Spherical or oval cavities formed in lava by gas bubbles.

Volcanic.   Rocks derived from magma erupting at the earth's surface.

Vug.   Small cavity in a rock, often of a mineral.

Appendix 2
Chemical Symbols and Names for Some Elements

Ag	silver	Mn	manganese
Al	aluminum	Mo	molybdenum
As	arsenic	Na	sodium
Au	gold	Nb	niobium
B	boron	Ni	nickel
Ba	barium	O	oxygen
Be	beryllium	P	phosphorus
Bi	bismuth	Pb	lead
C	carbon	Pd	palladium
Ca	calcium	Pt	platinum
Cb	columbium (niobium)	Rh	rhodium
Cd	cadmium	S	sulphur
Ce	cerium	Sb	antimony
Cl	chlorine	Se	selenium
Co	cobalt	Si	silicon
Cr	chromium	Sn	tin
Cs	cesium	Sr	strontium
Cu	copper	Ta	tantalum
Er	erbium	Te	tellurium
F	fluorine	Th	thorium
Fe	iron	Ti	titanium
H	hydrogen	U	uranium
Hf	hafnium	V	vanadium
Hg	mercury	W	tungsten
K	potassium	Y	yttrium
La	lanthanum	Yb	ytterbium
Li	lithium	Zn	zinc
Mg	magnesium	Zr	zirconium

Appendix 3
List of Minerals by Locality

The following are lists of the known minerals from each locality described in this book. For readers interested in acquiring further information about the areas and their respective mineralogy, references are given at the foot of each list (see bibliography for complete references).

Species	Chemical formula	Description
Klondike Area, Yukon		
casserite	SnO_2	brown, black bands; waterworn, rounded, massive; 2 cm
gold	Au	yellow, metallic; waterworn, massive, nuggets; 10 cm
hematite	Fe_2O_3	black, metallic; waterworn, rounded, massive; 3 cm

Sabina 1972, 103-7.

Species	Chemical formula	Description
Cassiar, British Columbia		
actinolite var nephrite	$Ca_2(Mg,Fe)_5Si_8O_{22}(OH)_2$	green; compact fibrous aggregations (jade)
antigorite	$(Mg,Fe)_3Si_2O_5(OH)_4$	green; fine-grained, massive, columnar
calcite	$CaCO_3$	white; columnar, cleavage masses; 10 cm
chlorite	$(Al,Fe,Li,Mg,Mn,Ni)_{5-6}$ $(Al,B,Fe,Si)_4O_{10}(OH)_8$	light green; fine-grained
chrysotile	$Mg_3Si_2O_5(OH)_4$	yellowish green; fibrous (asbestos); 4 cm
clinozoisite	$Ca_2Al_3(SiO_4)_3(OH)$	gray; columnar aggregates; 4 cm
grossular	$Ca_3Al_2(SiO_4)_3$	green; dodecahedral; 2 mm
lizardite	$Mg_3Si_2O_5(OH)_4$	green; fine-grained, massive
magnesite	$MgCO_3$	white; fibrous, columnar, splintery; 15 cm
magnetite	Fe_3O_4	black; anhedral grains
talc	$Mg_3Si_4O_{10}(OH)_2$	light green; fine-grained, flaky
tremolite	$Ca_2(Mg,Fe)_5Si_8O_{22}(OH)_2$	white; fibrous aggregates; 10 cm

Sabina 1972, 26-7.

Rapid Creek, Yukon		
alluaudite	$(Na,Ca)_4Fe_4$ $(Mn,Fe,Mg)_8(PO_4)_{12}$	dark green; radiating, fibrous; 1 cm
anatase	TiO_2	yellow-brown; pyramidal; 1 mm
apatite (*see* fluorapatite and carbonate-fluorapatite)		
ankerite	$Ca(Fe,Mg,Mn)(CO_3)_2$	tan; platy rhombohdra; 5 mm
aragonite	$CaCO_3$	white; acicular, botryoidal aggregates; 1 mm
arrojadite	$KNa_4CaMn_4Fe_{10}Al$ $(PO_4)_{12}(OH,F)_2$	green, honey-brown; tabular; 1 cm
augelite	$Al_2(PO_4)(OH)_3$	white, emerald green; thick, tabular crystals; 3 cm
baricite	$(Mg,Fe)_3(PO_4)_2 \cdot 8H_2O$	blue; large, cleavable masses; 10 cm
barite	$BaSO_4$	colourless; tabular; 0.5 mm
brazilianite	$NaAl_3(PO_4)_2(OH)_4$	white, light green; thick, tabular; 5 mm
carbonate-fluorapatite	$Ca_5(PO_4,CO_3)_3F$	white; botryoidal crusts
childrenite	$FeAl(PO_4)(OH)_2 \cdot H_2O$	brown; radiating, prismatic; 1 cm
collinsite	$Ca(Mg,Fe)(PO_4)_2 \cdot 2H_2O$	white, light beige; radiating, spear-shaped; 1 cm
diadochite	$Fe_2(PO_4)(SO_4)(OH) \cdot 5H_2O$	yellow-brown; earthy, botryoidal
dypingite	$Mg_5(CO_3)_4(OH)_2 \cdot 5H_2O$	white; thin crusts, botryoidal
epsomite	$MgSO_4 \cdot 7H_2O$	white; thin crusts, botryoidal
fluorapatite	$Ca_5(PO_4)_3F$	colourless, white, purple; hexagonal prisms; 1 cm
garyansellite	$Mg_3(PO_4)_2 \cdot 3H_2O$	brown, bronze lustre; tabular; 2 mm

Species	Chemical formula	Description
goethite	$FeO(OH)$	black; thin coatings
gorceixite	$BaAl_3(PO_4)_2(OH)_5 \cdot H_2O$	creamy white; pseudo-hexagonal plates; 3 mm
gordonite	$MgAl_2(PO_4)_2(OH)_2 \cdot 8H_2O$	colourless; white; radiating, acicular; 2 mm
gormanite	$Fe_3Al_4(PO_4)_4(OH)_6 \cdot 2H_2O$	bluish green; fibrous, radiating; 1 cm
goyazite	$SrAl_3(PO_4)_2(OH)_5 \cdot H_2O$	white; pseudo-cubic rhombs; 7 mm
gypsum	$CaSO_4 \cdot 2H_2O$	white; thin coatings
halotrichite	$FeAl_2(SO_4)_4 \cdot 22H_2O$	white, yellow; crusts, botryoidal
hexahydrite	$MgSO_4 \cdot 6H_2O$	white; platy, fibrous; 0.5 mm
hydromagnesite	$Mg_5(CO_3)_4(OH)_2 \cdot 4H_2O$	white; thin crusts, botryoidal
jarosite	$KFe_3(SO_4)_2(OH)_6$	yellow; earthy, irregular grains; 0.3 mm
kryzhanovskite	$MnFe_2(PO_4)_2(OH)_2 \cdot H_2O$	brown, bronze lustre; thick tabular; 2 cm
kulanite	$Ba(Fe,Mn,Mg)_2Al_2$ $(PO_4)_3(OH)_3$	dark blue-green; rosettes, plates; 15 mm
lazulite	$MgAl_2(PO_4)_2(OH)_2$	dark greenish blue; platy, rosettes, complex blocky twins; 15 mm
ludlamite	$(Fe,Mg,Mn)_3(PO_4)_2 \cdot 4H_2O$	bright green; tabular; 5 mm
maricite	$NaFePO_4$	gray; radiating aggregates replacing nodules; 10 cm
messelite	$Ca_2(Fe,Mn)(PO_4)_2 \cdot 2H_2O$	cream white; fibrous, botryoidal; 15 mm
metavivianite	$Fe_3(PO_4)_2(OH)_x \cdot (8-x)H_2O$	green; bladed, large cleavable masses; 9 cm
nahpoite	Na_2HPO_4	white; earthy
natrojarosite	$NaFe_3(SO_4)_2(OH)_6$	yellow-orange, orange-brown; irregular masses and grains
nesquehonite	$Mg(HCO_3)(OH) \cdot 2H_2O$	colourless; bladed, radiating aggregates; 5 mm
penikisite	$Ba(Mg,Fe)_2Al_2(PO_4)_3$ $(OH)_3$	blue, green; microscopic zones in kulanite
phosphosiderite	$FePO_4 \cdot 2H_2O$	yellow; prismatic; 1 cm
pyrite	FeS_2	brassy yellow; octahedral, cubic; 1 cm
quartz	SiO_2	colourless, white; prismatic; 10 cm
rapidcreekite	$Ca_2(SO_4)(CO_3) \cdot 4H_2O$	white; radiating needles; 3 mm
satterlyite	$(Fe,Mg)_2(PO_4)(OH)$	yellow-brown; radiating aggregates replacing nodules; 10 cm
siderite	$FeCO_3$	brown; rhombohedral, prismatic, scalenohedral; 2 cm
souzalite	$(Mg,Fe)_3(Al,Fe)_4(PO_4)_4$ $(OH)_6 \cdot 2H_2O$	dark bluish green; fibrous; radiating; 1 cm
sphalerite	$(Zn,Fe)S$	brown; anhedral masses and crystals; 3 cm
vivianite	$Fe_3(PO_4)_2 \cdot 8H_2O$	blue, blue-green; prismatic, bladed; 5 mm
wardite	$NaAl_3(PO_4)_2(OH)_4 \cdot 2H_2O$	white, pale green; pyramidal; 2 cm

Species	Chemical formula	Description
whiteite	$Ca(Fe,Mn)Mg_2Al_2(PO_4)_4$ $(OH)_2 \cdot 8H_2O$	beige; twinned, blocky crystals and sheaf-like aggregates; 2 cm
wicksite	$NaCa_2(Fe,Mn)_4MgFe$ $(PO_4)_6 \cdot H_2O$	dark blue, black; cleavage plates in nodules; 1 cm
wolfeite	$(Fe,Mn)_2(PO_4)(OH)$	brown, red; radiating aggregates replacing nodules; 10 cm

Coleman, Robertson 1981, 373-6; Mandarino, Sturman 1976, 127-31; Mandarino et al. 1977, 393-5; Mandarino et al. 1978, 411-13; Roberts et al. 1985; Robertson 1982, 177-87; Sturman, Dunn 1984, 207-9; Sturman, Mandarino 1976, 403-6; Sturman et al. 1977, 396-8; Sturman et al. 1981a, 377-80; Sturman et al. 1981b, 381-7.

Rock Candy Mine, British Columbia

barite	$BaSO_4$	golden yellow, colourless, gray; tabular; 10 cm
fluorite	CaF_2	green, colourless, purple; octahedral, cubic, stepped growth; 12 cm
quartz	SiO_2	white; short prismatic, drusy coatings; 2 mm

Nagel 1981, 99-101.

Drumheller, Alberta

aragonite	$CaCO_3$	green, red, beige; iridescent crusts on fossil ammonites
calcite	$CaCO_3$	white, yellowish; rhombohedral, scalenohedral; 5 mm
quartz	SiO_2	colourless; short prismatic, pyramidal terminations; 1 mm
quartz, chalcedony	SiO_2	white, gray; botryoidal, fine-grained replacement of dinosaur bones and wood fragments

Esterhazy, Saskatchewan

anhydrite	$CaSO_4$	white to gray; granular
carnallite	$KMgCl_3 \cdot 6H_2O$	white, red, black; granular, cleavages; 10 cm
dolomite	$CaMg(CO_3)_2$	buff to red; granular
halite	$NaCl$	colourless, white, gray, blue; massive, cleavages; 10 cm
sylvite	KCl	white, pink, light orange; massive, cleavages; 1 cm

Holter 1969.

Winnipeg, Manitoba

gypsum	$CaSO_4 \cdot 2H_2O$	pale yellow, amber; lenticular, rosettes; 6 cm

Species	Chemical formula	Description
Bernic Lake, Manitoba		
albite	$NaAlSi_3O_8$	colourless, gray; radiating plates; 5 cm
amblygonite	$(Li,Na)Al(PO_4)(F,OH)$	white, yellow, pink; prismatic; 40 cm
analcime	$NaAlSi_2O_6 \cdot H_2O$	colourless, white, brownish; trapezohedral; 2 mm
antimony	Sb	tin-white, metallic; fine-grained aggregates
arsenic	As	tin-white, metallic; fine-grained aggregates
arsenopyrite	$FeAsS$	silver-white, metallic; prismatic; 2 cm
barite	$BaSO_4$	colourless; prismatic; 0.5 mm
beryl	$Be_3Al_2Si_6O_{18}$	colourless, white, pale pink; hexagonal prisms; 13 cm
bismuth	Bi	silver-white, metallic; fine-grained aggregates
bournonite	$PbCuSbS_3$	gray, metallic; minute grains
calcite	$CaCO_3$	colourless, light pink; irregular masses
cassiterite	SnO_2	black; fine-grained
cernyite	Cu_2CdSnS_4	gray, metallic; minute grains
cesstibtantite	$(Cs,Na,Sb)Ta_2(O,OH)_7$	orange-yellow; cubo-octahedral; 0.1 mm
chalcopyrite	$CuFeS_2$	brassy yellow, metallic; fine-grained aggregates
cookeite	$LiAl_4(Si_3Al)O_{10}(OH)_8$	white, pink, greenish; flakes; 2 mm
cosalite	$Pb_2Bi_2S_5$	gray, metallic; minute grains
crandallite	$CaAl_3(PO_4)_2(OH)_5 \cdot H_2O$	yellowish white; spongy replacement
cubanite	$CuFe_2S_3$	bronzy yellow, metallic; irregular grains
diomignite	$Li_2B_4O_7$	colourless; equidimensional; 0.03 mm
dorfmanite	$Na_2HPO_4 \cdot 2H_2O$	white; powder
dyscrasite	Ag_3Sb	silver-white, metallic; fine-grained aggregates
eucryptite	$LiAlSiO_4$	gray, pink; irregular grains; 4 cm
fairfieldite	$Ca_2(Mn,Fe)(PO_4)_2 \cdot 2H_2O$	white; platy, acicular, radiating, massive; 1 mm
ferrocolumbite	$(Fe,Mn)(Nb,Ta)_2O_6$	black; prismatic grains; 1 mm
ferrotapiolite	$FeTa_2O_6$	black; minute grains
fluorapatite	$Ca_5(PO_4)_3F$	brown, pink, blue; fine-grained aggregates, massive
freibergite	$(Ag,Cu,Fe)_{12}(Sb,As)_4S_{13}$	gray, metallic; minute grains
galena	PbS	lead-gray, metallic; minute grains
gladite	$PbCuBi_5S_9$	gray, metallic; prismatic; 4 cm
gustavite	$PbAgBi_3S_6$	gray, metallic; irregular grains; 2 mm
hawleyite	CdS	yellow; minute grains
holmquistite	$Li_2(Mg,Fe)_3Al_2Si_8O_{22}(OH)_2$	blue; fibrous aggregates
illite	$(K,H_3O)(Al,Mg,Fe)_2(Si,Al)_4O_{10}[(OH)_2H_2O]$	white, pale green; radiating fibres, globular aggregates

Species	Chemical formula	Description
ilmenite	$FeTiO_3$	brown; fine-grained
ixiolite	$(Ta,Nb,Sn,Fe,Mn)_4O_8$	black; platy; 10 mm
kesterite	$Cu_2(Zn,Fe)SnS_4$	greenish black; minute grains
lead	Pb	gray, metallic; minute grains
lepidolite	$K(Li,Al)_3(Si,Al)_4O_{10}$ $(F,OH)_2$	purple; fine-grained, micaceous
lithiophilite-triphylite	$LiMnPO_4 \cdot LiFePO_4$	brown, yellowish brown; resinous; irregular masses; 4 cm
lithiophosphate	Li_3PO_4	pale beige, silky; irregular etched masses; 5 cm
manganocolumbite	$Mn(Nb,Ta)_2O_6$	black; prismatic, grains; 1 mm
manganotantalite	$MnTa_2O_6$	black; prismatic, grains; 2 cm
marcasite	FeS_2	brassy yellow; botryoidal crusts
miargyrite	$AgSbS_2$	gray, metallic; minute grains
microcline	$KAlSi_3O_8$	white, gray, beige, pink; cleavage masses; 250 cm
microlite	$(Na,Ca)_2Ta_2O_6(O,OH,F)$	pale yellow; irregular grains; 1 mm
molybdenite	MoS_2	lead-gray, metallic; flakes
montebrasite	$LiAlPO_4(OH)$	white, brown, gray, greenish; prismatic, irregular masses; 40 cm
montmorillonite	$(Na,Ca)_{0.33}(Al,Mg)_2Si_4O_{10}$ $(OH)_2 \cdot nH_2O$	white, pale green; radiating fibres, globular aggregates
muscovite	$KAl_2(Si_3Al)O_{10}(OH, F)_2$	white, greenish; fine-grained, micaceous
overite	$CaMgAl(PO_4)_2(OH)$ $\cdot 4H_2O$	colourless; stacked, tabular; 0.5 mm
pekoite	$PbCuBi_{11}(S,Se)_{18}$	gray, metallic; prismatic; 4 cm
petalite	$LiAlSi_4O_{10}$	white, gray; prismatic, tabular; 200 cm
pollucite	$(Cs,Na)_2Al_2Si_4O_{12} \cdot H_2O$	colourless, white; irregular masses; 200 cm
pyrargyrite	Ag_3SbS_3	red; minute grains
pyrite	FeS_2	brassy yellow; botryoidal crusts, fine-grained aggregates
pyrrhotite	$Fe_{1-x}S$	bronzy yellow, metallic; irregular grains
quartz	SiO_2	colourless, white, gray; striated hexagonal prisms, rhombohedral terminations
rhodochrosite	$MnCO_3$	salmon-pink; granular; 5 mm
sanidine	$KAlSi_3O_8$	colourless; radiating tabular aggregates, fine-grained; 1 mm
schorl	$NaFe_3Al_6(BO_3)_3Si_6O_{18}$ $(OH)_4$	black; prismatic; 20 cm
simpsonite	$Al_4(Ta,Nb)_3O_{13}(OH)$	colourless, pale pink; hexagonal prisms; 1 cm

Species	Chemical formula	Description
sphalerite	$(Zn,Fe)S$	yellow, brown; anhedral grains
spodumene	$LiAlSi_2O_6$	colourless, greenish; columnar, bladed, prismatic aggregates; 150 cm
stannite	Cu_2FeSnS_4	gray, metallic; minute grains
stibarsen	$SbAs$	tin-white, metallic; fine-grained aggregates
switzerite	$(Mn,Fe)_3(PO_4)_2 \cdot 4H_2O$	bronze; platy, scaly aggregates
tancoite	$HNa_2LiAl(PO_4)_2(OH)$	colourless, pale pink; equant to tabular, parallel growth; 1 mm
Ta-richwodginite	$Mn_2Ta_{12}O_{32}$	yellow-orange; clusters of subparallel plates; 1 cm
tetrahedrite	$(Cu,Fe)_{12}Sb_4S_{13}$	gray, metallic; minute grains
thorite	$ThSiO_4$	brown; minute blebs
titanowodginite	$Mn_4Ti_4Ta_8O_{32}$	black; diamond-shaped, penetration twins; 1 cm
uraninite	UO_2	black; cubic; 1 mm
uranmicrolite	$(U,Ca,Na)_{2-x}Ta_2O_6(OH,F)_y$	dark brown; irregular grains; 2 mm
whitlockite	$Ca_9(Mg,Fe)H(PO_4)_7$	colourless; rhombohedral; 1 mm
wodginite	$(Ta,Nb,Sn,Mn,Fe)_{16}O_{32}$	brown, black; prismatic, skeletal, wedge-shaped, fine-grained; 4 mm
zircon	$ZrSiO_4$	pink, brown; pyramidal, fine-grained aggregates; 1 mm

Cerny 1982, 527-43; Ercit et al. 1984, 502; Kissin et al. 1978, 139-46; London et al. 1987, 173-80; Nickel et al. 1963, 390-402; Ramik et al. 1980, 185-90.

Species	Chemical formula	Description
Thunder Bay Area, Ontario		
barite	$BaSO_4$	white, creamy, rusty, orange; bladed; 10 cm
calcite	$CaCo_3$	white, creamy; scalenohedral, blocky, rhombohedral; 30 cm
chalcopyrite	$CuFeS_2$	brassy yellow, metallic; pyramidal; 1 cm
fluorite	CaF_2	pale green; cubic; 4 cm
galena	PbS	lead-gray, metallic; cubic cleavages; 1 cm
goethite	$FeO(OH)$	brown; acicular, radiating; 2 mm
hematite	Fe_2O_3	red; thin coatings, spherical aggregates; 0.5 mm
malachite	$Cu_2(CO_3)(OH)_2$	green; thin coatings
marcasite	FeS_2	brassy yellow; tabular; 1 mm
pyrite	FeS_2	brassy yellow, metallic; cubic, octahedral; 1 mm
quartz	SiO_2	colourless to deep purple (amethyst); short prismatic, pyramidal terminations; 60 cm
silver	Ag	silver-white; wires; 1 mm
sphalerite	$(Zn,Fe)S$	brown, resinous; cleavages; 2 cm

Elliot 1982, 67-70; Kile 1984, 262-271.

Species	Chemical formula	Description
Wawa, Ontario		
anatase	TiO_2	black, gray, glassy; blunt pyramids, tetragonal plates; 1 mm
calcite	$CaCO_3$	colourless, white; rhombohedral, scalenohedral, prismatic, parallel and subparallel growth; 4 cm
copiapite	$Fe_5(SO_4)_6(OH)_2 \cdot 20H_2O$	yellow; botryoidal crusts
dolomite	$CaMg(CO_3)_2$	white, yellowish; rhombohedral; 1 cm
galena	PbS	lead-gray, metallic; cleavages; 2 cm
goethite	$FeO(OH)$	yellowish brown, dark brown; radiating fibrous, botryoidal; 5 mm
gypsum	$CaSO_4 \cdot 2H_2O$	colourless; tabular, diamond-shaped; 4 cm
hematite	Fe_2O_3	black; platy, rosettes; 15 mm
marcasite	FeS_2	brassy yellow; tabular, curved, cockscomb twins; 3 cm
pyrite	FeS_2	brassy yellow; cubic, cubo-octahedral, subparallel aggregates; 3 cm
quartz	SiO_2	colourless, smoky; short prismatic, pyramidal terminations; 2 cm
siderite	$FeCO_3$	light brown; rhombohedral; 2 mm

Species	Chemical formula	Description
Sudbury Area, Ontario		
altaite	PbTe	tin-white, metallic; grains
annabergite	$Ni_3(AsO_4)_2 \cdot 8H_2O$	green; crusts
argentopentlandite	$Ag(Fe,Ni)_8S_8$	red (in polished section); grains; 0.5 mm
arsenohauchecornite	Ni_9BiAsS_8	bronze, metallic; irregular grains; 1 mm
bismuth	Bi	silver-white, metallic; irregular grains; 0.7 mm
bornite	Cu_5FeS_4	bronze, iridescent purple tarnish; irregular masses
breithauptite	NiSb	copper-red, metallic; grains
brucite	$Mg(OH)_2$	gray; aggregates of rounded grains; 2 mm
chalcanthite	$CuSO_4 \cdot 5H_2O$	blue; crusts
chalcopyrite	$CuFeS_2$	brassy yellow, metallic; pyramidal crystals, irregular masses; 1 cm
cobaltite	CoAsS	tin-white, metallic; irregular grains; 5 mm
copper	Cu	copper-red, metallic; arborescent; 2 mm
cubanite	$CuFe_2S_3$	bronzy yellow, metallic; thick tabular, twinned, irregular masses; 1 cm
erythrite	$Co_3(AsO_4)_2 \cdot 8H_2O$	pink; crusts
froodite	$PdBi_2$	gray, metallic; irregular grains; 0.1 mm
galena	PbS	lead-gray, metallic; cubic, cleavage fragments; 1 cm
gersdorffite	NiAsS	tin-white, metallic; granular; 5 mm
gold	Au	yellow, metallic; irregular grains; 5 mm
hematite	Fe_2O_3	black; platy, earthy
hessite	Ag_2Te	steel-gray, metallic; anhedral grains; 0.2 mm
ilmenite	$FeTiO_3$	black, metallic; tabular, irregular grains; 3 cm
insizwaite	$Pt(Bi,Sb)S_2$	tin-white, metallic; irregular grains; 0.1 mm
kotulskite	Pd(Te,Bi)	creamy white, metallic; anhedral grains; 0.05 mm
mackinawite	$(Fe,Ni)_9S_8$	bronze, gray, metallic; grains
magnetite	Fe_3O_4	black, metallic; octahedral, anhedral grains; 4 mm
malachite	$Cu_2(CO_3)(OH)_2$	green; crusts
marcasite	FeS_2	brassy yellow, metallic; bladed, nodular, fine-grained
matildite	$AgBiS_2$	lead-gray, metallic; anhedral grain; 0.2 mm
maucherite	$Ni_{11}As_8$	steel-gray, purple tarnish; fine-grained, massive; 5 mm
melanterite	$FeSO_4 \cdot 7H_2O$	bluish white; crusts
melonite-Pd	$(Ni,Pd)Te_2$	reddish white, metallic; grains

Species	Chemical formula	Description
merenskyite	$(Pd,Pt)(Te,Bi)_2$	tin-white, metallic; irregular grains; 0.1 mm
mertieite-II	$Pd_8(Sb,As)_3$	creamy yellow, metallic; irregular grains; 0.03 mm
michenerite	$(Pd,Pt)BiTe$	grayish white, metallic; fine-grained
millerite	NiS	brassy yellow, metallic; fibrous, radiating, cleavages; 3 cm
moncheite	$(Pt,Pd)(Te,Bi)_2$	steel-gray, metallic; irregular grains; 0.2 mm
morenosite	$NiSO_4 \cdot 7H_2O$	green; crusts
nickeline	$NiAs$	pale copper-red, metallic; fine-grained, massive, 1 mm
niggliite	$PtSn$	creamy pink, blue (in polished section); anhedral grains; 0.02 mm
parkerite	$Ni_3(Bi,Pb)_2S_2$	bronze, metallic; irregular grains; 3 mm
pentlandite	$(Fe,Ni)_9S_8$	bronzy yellow, metallic; irregular masses; 5 cm
polydymite	$NiNi_2S_4$	gray, metallic; fine-grained
pyrite	FeS_2	brassy yellow, metallic; cubic, octahedral, irregular grains; 1 cm
pyrrhotite	$Fe_{1-x}S$	bronzy yellow, metallic; irregular masses; 3 cm
silver	Ag	silver-white, metallic; thin veins, irregular grains; 1 cm
sperrylite	$PtAs_2$	tin-white, metallic; cubic, cubo-octahedral; 1 cm
sphalerite	$(Zn,Fe)S$	brown; fine-grained; 1 mm
stannite	Cu_2FeSnS_4	brownish gray, metallic; fine-grained; 0.1 mm
sudburyite	$(Pd,Ni)Sb$	tin-white, metallic; elongate grains; 0.1 mm
tetradymite	Bi_2Te_2S	pale steel-gray; irregular grains; 0.05 mm
valleriite	$4(Fe,Cu)S \cdot 3(Mg,Al)(OH)_2$	pale bronze-yellow, metallic; thin fibres; 0.1 mm
violarite	Ni_2FeS_4	steel-gray, metallic; fine-grained
wehrlite	$BiTe(?)$	lead-gray, metallic; grains

Cabri, Laflamme 1976, 1159-95; Gait, Harris 1980, 877-8; Hawley, Stanton 1962, 30-145; Naldrett 1984, 309-25.

Species	Chemical formula	Description
Cobalt Area, Ontario		
acanthite	Ag_2S	black, metallic; pseudomorphs after cubic and octahedral argentite, massive, grains; 3 cm
actinolite	$Ca_2(Mg,Fe)_5Si_8O_{22}(OH)_2$	pale green; minute needles
albite	$NaAlSi_3O_8$	white, pink; massive
allanite	$(Ce,Ca,Y)_2(Al,Fe)_3$ $(SiO_4)_3(OH)$	dark brown; minute needles
allargentum	$Ag_{1-x}Sb_x$	silver, metallic; lamellar intergrowths with silver, veinlets, grains
alloclasite	$(Co,Fe)AsS$	steel-gray, metallic; prismatic, massive
anatase	TiO_2	black; grains
annabergite	$Ni_3(AsO_4)_2 \cdot 8H_2O$	light green; crusts
apatite	$Ca_5(PO_4)_3(F,Cl,OH)$	yellow, colourless; prismatic; 3 mm
arsenic	As	tin-white, metallic, tarnishes; grains.
arsenopyrite	$FeAsS$	silver-white, gray, metallic; prismatic, botryoidal masses, veinlets; 1 cm
axinite	$(Ca,Fe,Mg,Mn)_3$ $Al_2BSi_4O_{15}OH$	purple, greenish brown; wedge-shaped, massive; 1 cm
barite	$BaSO_4$	orange; massive.
bismuth	Bi	silver-white, metallic, tarnishes; cleavage masses, veinlets, grains
bismuthinite	Bi_2S_3	tin-white, gray, metallic, tarnishes; grains, veinlets.
bornite	Cu_5FeS_4	copper-red, metallic, tarnishes purple; grains, veinlets
bravoite	$(Ni,Fe)S_2$	steel-gray, metallic; thin layers in pyrite grains
breithauptite	$NiSb$	pale copper-red, metallic; fine-grained intergrowths with nickeline
calcite	$CaCO_3$	colourless, white, gray; fine to medium-grained, scalenohedral, rhombohedral; 15 mm
cerite	$(Ce,Ca)_9(Mg,Fe)Si_7$ $(O,OH,F)_{28}$	pale pink; fine grained
chalcocite	Cu_2S	black, metallic; grains, intergrowths, veinlets
chalcopyrite	$CuFeS_2$	brassy yellow, metallic; massive, botryoidal aggregates, grains, veinlets
chlorite	$(Al,Fe,Li,Mg,Mn,Ni)_{5-6}$ $(Al,B,Fe,Si)_4O_{10}(OH)_8$	green, greenish black; radiating sheaves, spheroids
chromite	$FeCr_2O_4$	black; overgrowth on magnetite grains
clinosafflorite	$(Co,Fe,Ni)As_2$	tin-white, metallic; intergrowths with skutterudite

Species	Chemical formula	Description
cobaltite	$CoAsS$	tin-white, metallic; octahedral, layers in arsenide rosettes, grains; 7 mm
cobaltpentlandite	Co_9S_8	bronzy yellow, metallic; veinlets, grains
covellite	CuS	dark blue; thin coatings
dolomite	$CaMg(CO_3)_2$	pinkish white; fine-grained
dyscrasite	Ag_3Sb	silver-white; intergrowths with allargentum
epidote	$Ca_2(Al,Fe)_3(SiO_4)_3(OH)$	apple-green; fine-grained
erythrite	$Co_3(AsO_4)_2 \cdot 8H_2O$	pink to rose; radiating fibrous sprays, crusts; 1 mm
freieslebenite	$AgPbSbS_3$	silver-white, gray, metallic; minute veinlet
galena	PbS	lead-gray, metallic; cubo-octahedral, cleavage masses, grains; 5 mm
galenobismutite	$PbBi_2S_4$	tin-white, gray, metallic; platy, veinlets
gersdorffite	$NiAsS$	tin-white, metallic, tarnishes; massive, grains
glaucodot	$(Co,Fe)AsS$	tin-white, metallic; fine-grained intergrowth with alloclasite and arsenopyrite
hematite	Fe_2O_3	reddish brown; minute grains
ilmenite	$FeTiO_3$	black; grains
langisite	$(Co,Ni)As$	pinkish buff, metallic; veinlets, grains, lamellae
larosite	$(Cu,Ag)_{21}(Pb,Bi)_2S_{13}$	whitish buff; acicular; 0.3 mm
loellingite	$FeAs_2$	silver-white, gray, metallic; layers in rosette-like masses, star-shaped grains
magnetite	Fe_3O_4	black; fine-grained
marcasite	FeS_2	brassy yellow, metallic; massive, grains, veinlets
matildite	$AgBiS_2$	gray, black, metallic; lamellar and irregular intergrowths in galena and pavonite
maucherite	$Ni_{11}As_8$	silver-gray, metallic, tarnishes; grains, radiating fibrous aggregates
mckinstryite	$(Ag,Cu)_2S$	steel-gray, metallic, tarnishes; coarse-grained aggregates; 3 mm
millerite	NiS	bronzy yellow, metallic; fibrous
molybdenite	MoS_2	lead-gray, metallic; minute flakes
nickeline	$NiAs$	pale copper-red, metallic; layers in botryoidal and rosette-like masses, grains
pararammelsbergite	$NiAs_2$	tin-white, metallic; prismatic, intergrowths with arsenides, grains
parkerite	$Ni_3(Bi,Pb)_2S_2$	cream-white, metallic; minute intergrowths with bismuth and bismuthinite
pavonite	$(Ag,Cu)(Bi,Pb)_3S_5$	tin-white, gray, metallic; veinlets

Species	Chemical formula	Description
pearceite	$Ag_{16}As_2S_{11}$	black; platy
polybasite	$(Ag,Cu)_{16}Sb_2S_{11}$	black; platy
proustite	Ag_3AsS_3	red, adamantine; prismatic, scalenohedral, grains; 3 mm
pyrargyrite	Ag_3SbS_3	deep red; stubby prismatic, massive, veinlets, grains; 8 mm
pyrite	FeS_2	brassy yellow, metallic; nodules, grains; 1 cm
pyrrhotite	$Fe_{1-x}S$	bronze, metallic; massive, intergrowths, grains
quartz	SiO_2	colourless, white; short prismatic, massive; 3 mm
rammelsbergite	$NiAs_2$	tin-white, metallic; radiating fibrous aggregates, layers in botryoidal masses, grains
rutile	TiO_2	black; grains
safflorite	$CoAs_2$	tin-white, gray tarnish, metallic; radiating fibrous aggregates, irregular grains
samsonite	$Ag_4MnSb_2S_6$	black, metallic; grains
siegenite	$(Ni,Co)_3S_4$	gray, metallic, tarnishes; grains
silver	Ag	silver-white, gray to black tarnish, metallic; sheets, wires, veinlets, grains, dendrites
skutterudite	$CoAs_{2-3}$	tin-white, metallic; cubic, layers in arsenide rosettes, dendritic; 2 cm
smythite	$(Fe,Ni)_9S_{11}$	black, metallic; grains
sphalerite	$(Zn,Fe)S$	brown, black; rounded, cleavage masses, grains
stephanite	Ag_5SbS_4	black, metallic; short prismatic, tabular, veinlets, grains, intergrowths; 5 mm
stilpnomelane	$K(Fe,Al)_{10}Si_{12}O_{30}(OH)_{12}$	brown; flakes
stromeyerite	$AgCuS$	steel-gray, metallic, tarnishes blue; grains, intergrowths
tetrahedrite	$(Cu,Fe)_{12}Sb_4S_{13}$	gray, black, metallic; massive, grains, veinlets
titanite	$CaTiSiO_5$	green; minute grains
ullmannite	$NiSbS$	tin-white, gray, metallic; grains
violarite	Ni_2FeS_4	gray, metallic, tarnishes; grains
wittichenite	Cu_3BiS_3	steel-gray, tin-white, metallic, tarnishes; grains
wolframite	$(Mn,Fe)WO_4$	black; minute grains
xanthoconite	Ag_3AsS_3	orange, brown; fine-grained intergrowths with sphalerite and siderite, pyramidal and tabular crystals; 1 mm

Jambor 1971, 232-61; Petruk 1971, 108-36; Petruk 1972, 886-91; Petruk et al. 1969, 597-616; Petruk et al. 1971a, 150-86; Petruk et al. 1971b, 187-94; Petruk et al. 1971c, 196-227; Sabina 1974; Skinner et al. 1966, 1383-9.

Species	Chemical formula	Description
Bancroft Area, Ontario		
actinolite	$Ca_2(Mg,Fe)_5Si_8O_{22}(OH)_2$	green, black; long to short prismatic; 20 cm
albite	$NaAlSi_3O_8$	white, gray, brown, blue schiller (peristerite); blocky, short prismatic, cleavage masses; 20 cm
allanite	$(Ce,Ca,Y)_2(Al,Fe)_3$ $(SiO_4)_3(OH)$	brown, black; tabular; 30 cm
analcime	$NaAlSi_2O_6 \cdot H_2O$	white; massive
anatase	TiO_2	black, brown; fine-grained replacement of ilmenite
anhydrite	$CaSO_4$	purple, green, blue; cleavage masses; 20 cm
apatite (*see* fluorapatite)		
aragonite	$CaCO_3$	white; nodules; 3 mm
augite	$(Ca,Na)(Mg,Fe,Al,Ti)$ $(Si,Al)_2O_6$	black; stout prismatic; 4 cm
betafite	$(Ca,Na,U)_2(Ti,Nb,Ta)_2$ $O_6(OH)$	brown; cubo-octahedral, irregular masses; 7 cm
biotite	$K(Mg,Fe)_3(Al,Fe)Si_3O_{10}$ $(OH,F)_2$	black; tapering hexagonal-shaped prisms, micaceous; 120 cm
boehmite	$AlO(OH)$	white; powder, fibrous, fine-grained aggregates
brucite	$Mg(OH)_2$	white; nodules; 3 mm
brugnatellite	$Mg_6Fe(CO_3)(OH)_{13} \cdot 4H_2O$	white; compact nodules; 3 mm
calcite	$CaCO_3$	colourless, blue, white, salmon-pink, honey-yellow; scalenohedral, rhombohedral, twins, cleavage masses; 30 cm
cancrinite	$Na_6Ca_2Al_6Si_6O_{24}(CO_3)_2$	pink, white, yellow, light green; cleavage masses; 10 cm
celestite	$SrSO_4$	light brown; acicular; 2 cm
chabazite	$CaAl_2Si_4O_{12} \cdot 6H_2O$	golden to dark brown; twinned, lenticular; 15 mm
chalcopyrite	$CuFeS_2$	brassy yellow, metallic; elongate inclusions in calcite, pyramidal; 15 mm
chlorite group	$(Al,Fe,Li,Mg,Mn,Ni)_{5-6}$ $(Al,B,Fe,Si)_4O_{10}(OH)_8$	green; platy, micaceous; 5 cm
chondrodite	$(Mg,Fe)_5(SiO_4)_2(F,OH)_2$	brown; irregular masses, grains; 5 mm
clinohumite	$(Mg,Fe)_9(SiO_4)_4(F,OH)_2$	brownish yellow; grains
corundum	Al_2O_3	gray, blue, black; tapering barrel-shaped prisms; 15 cm
datolite	$CaBSiO_4(OH)$	colourless, pale green; short prismatic; 3 cm

Species	Chemical formula	Description
dawsonite	$NaAl(CO_3)(OH)_2$	colourless, white, silky; fibrous aggregates, striated masses; 1 mm
diopside	$CaMgSi_2O_6$	brown; prismatic, blocky, cleavage masses; 30 cm
dravite	$NaMg_3Al_6(BO_3)_3Si_6O_{18}(OH)_4$	black; short prismatic; 9 cm
epidote	$Ca_2(Al,Fe)_3(SiO_4)_3(OH)$	light green; acicular sprays; 0.1 mm
euxenite	$(Y,Ca,Ce,U,Th)(Nb,Ta,Ti)_2O_6$	black, brown; irregular masses
fluoborite	$Mg_3(BO_3)(F,OH)_3$	colourless, light pink; hexagonal prisms; 2 mm
fluorapatite	$Ca_5(PO_4)_3F$	green, brownish green; hexagonal prisms; 60 cm
fluorite	CaF_2	purple, green; octahedral, granular aggregates; 14 mm
forsterite	Mg_2SiO_4	pink, yellow, brown, colourless; tabular, irregular masses, grains 2 cm
galena	PbS	lead-gray, metallic; cleavage masses; 2 cm
goethite	$FeO(OH)$	black; powder, crusts
graphite	C	black, metallic; nodules, irregular flakes; 1 cm
grossular	$Ca_3Al_2(SiO_4)_3$	brown, brownish orange; dodecahedral; 7 cm
gypsum	$CaSO_4 \cdot 2H_2O$	colourless; thick tabular; 100 cm
hematite	Fe_2O_3	black; botryoidal, crusts; 1 cm
hornblende	$Ca_2(Fe,Mg)_4Al(Si_7Al)O_{22}(OH,F)_2$	black; short prismatic, blocky, cleavage masses; 120 cm
humite	$(Mg,Fe)_7(SiO_4)_3(F,OH)_2$	brown; irregular masses; 2 cm
hydromagnesite	$Mg_5(CO_3)_4(OH)_2 \cdot 4H_2O$	creamy white, waxy; nodules, fibrous aggregates; 3 mm
hydrotalcite	$Mg_6Al_2(CO_3)(OH)_{16} \cdot 4H_2O$	white; nodules; 3 mm
hydroxylbastnaesite	$(Ce,La)(CO_3)(OH,F)$	brown, green, resinous, fine-grained
ilmenite	$FeTiO_3$	black; tabular; 35 cm
kainosite	$Ca_2(Y,Ce)_2Si_4O_{12}(CO_3) \cdot H_2O$	tan; radiating acicular, square prisms; 1 cm
kyanite	Al_2SiO_5	gray; compact fibrous aggregates; 3 mm
lepidocrocite	$FeO(OH)$	brown; thin scales
ludwigite	Mg_2FeBO_5	black; striated prisms, nodules; 2 mm
magnetite	Fe_3O_4	black; octahedral; 25 cm
marcasite	FeS_2	brassy yellow, metallic; bladed; 2 mm
meionite	$3CaAl_2Si_2O_8 \cdot CaCO_3$	gray, greenish white, greenish yellow; tetragonal prisms, massive; 17 cm

Species	Chemical formula	Description
melanocerite	$(Ce,Ca)_5(Si,B)_3O_{12}(OH,F)$ $\cdot nH_2O$	brown, resinous; massive
microcline	$KAlSi_3O_8$	white, gray, brown, pink, green (amazonite); blocky, short prismatic, cleavage masses; 90 cm
molybdenite	MoS_2	lead-gray, metallic; irregular flakes; 2 cm
monazite	$(Ce,La,Nd,Th)PO_4$	brown; tabular; 2 cm
monticellite	$CaMgSiO_4$	colourless, greenish to yellowish gray; grains; 1 mm
muscovite	$KAl_2(Si_3Al)O_{10}(OH,F)_2$	light gray; tabular, diamond-shaped, micaceous, 15 cm
natrolite	$Na_2Al_2Si_3O_{10}\cdot2H_2O$	colourless, white, orange-red; prismatic, radiating aggregates; 2 cm
nepheline	$(Na,K)AlSiO_4$	gray; short hexagonal prisms; 25 cm
nordstrandite	$Al(OH)_3$	colourless; bladed; 1 mm
oligoclase	$(Na,Ca)Al(Al,Si)Si_2O_8$	white, gray, blue schiller (peristerite); blocky, short prismatic, tabular, cleavage masses; 25 cm
orthoclase	$KAlSi_3O_8$	brown; blocky, short prismatic; 20 cm
pectolite	$NaCa_2Si_3O_8(OH)$	white; acicular; 1 mm
periclase	MgO	amber; grains
perovskite	$CaTiO_3$	black; octahedral; 2 mm
perrierite	$(Ca,Ce,Th)_4(Mg,Fe)_2$ $(Ti,Fe)_3Si_4O_{22}$	reddish brown, resinous, platy, irregular masses; 2 mm
phlogopite	$KMg_3Si_3AlO_{10}(F,OH)_2$	brown; short hexagonal-shaped prisms, micaceous, 15 cm
pyrite	FeS_2	brassy yellow, metallic; cubic; 3 mm
pyrrhotite	$Fe_{1-x}S$	bronzy yellow; irregular masses; 3 cm
quartz	SiO_2	white, smoky; prismatic, massive; 7 cm
rozenite	$FeSO_4\cdot4H_2O$	white; powder
rutile	TiO_2	brown, black; irregular blebs; 1 cm
scapolite (*see* meionite)		
schorl	$NaFe_3Al_6(BO_3)_3Si_6O_{18}$ $(OH)_4$	black; prismatic; 2 cm
sepiolite	$Mg_4Si_6O_{15}(OH)_2\cdot6H_2O$	white, light amber; matted fibrous aggregates
serpentine group	$(Mg,Fe,Ni)_3Si_2O_5(OH)_4$	green, brown, resinous; granular, nodular
sinhalite	$MgAlBO_4$	colourless; sugary crusts on spinel
sodalite	$Na_8Al_6Si_6O_{24}Cl_2$	blue, white to pink (hackmanite); cleavage masses; 10 cm

Species	Chemical formula	Description
spinel	$MgAl_2O_4$	black, green, mauve; octahedral; 12 mm
stillwellite	$(Ce,La,Ca)BSiO_5$	maroon-red, gray, pink; tabular, lenticular, irregular masses; 5 mm
szaibelyite	$MgBO_2(OH)$	buff; fine-grained crusts, nodules
szomolnokite	$FeSO_4 \cdot H_2O$	white; powder
thorianite	ThO_2	black; irregular masses; 15 mm
thorite	$ThSiO_4$	black (uranium-bearing), brown, red, orange; short tetragonal prisms, pyramidal, grains; 8 cm
titanite	$CaTiSiO_5$	black, brown; wedge-shaped; 10 cm
tochilinite	$6Fe_{0.9}S\text{-}5(Mg,Fe)(OH)_2$	black, greasy; irregular patches, coatings
tremolite	$Ca_2(Mg,Fe)_5Si_8O_{22}(OH)_2$	green; long to short prismatic; 20 cm
tritomite-Y	$(Y,Ca,La,Fe)_5(Si,B,Al)_3 (O,OH,F)_{13}$	reddish brown, resinous; aggregates of tabular prisms, massive; 3 cm
uraninite	UO_2	grayish black; cubic, cubo-octahedral; 5 cm
uranophane	$Ca(UO_2)_2Si_2O_7 \cdot 5H_2O$	yellow; fibrous, radiating; 2 cm
uranophane-beta	$Ca(UO_2)_2Si_2O_7 \cdot 5H_2O$	yellow; acicular; 2 mm
uranopilite	$(UO_2)_6(SO_4)(OH)_{10} \cdot 12H_2O$	yellow; thin crusts
uranpyrochlore	$(U,Ca,Ce)_2(Nb,Ta)_2O_6 (OH,F)$	brown, black; rounded cubo-octahedra; 2 cm
vermiculite group	$(Mg,Fe,Al)_3(Al,Si)_4O_{10} (OH)_2 \cdot 4H_2O$	bronzy yellow; micaceous alteration of biotite
vesuvianite	$Ca_{10}Mg_2Al_4(SiO_4)_5 (Si_2O_7)_2(OH)_4$	brown, brownish yellow; tetragonal prisms; 2 cm
warwickite	$(Mg,Ti,Fe,Al)_2(BO_3)O$	black; prismatic, fine-grained aggregates; 2 mm
wollastonite	$CaSiO_3$	white; tabular, cleavage masses; 2 cm
zircon	$ZrSiO_4$	brown, pink; tetragonal prisms; 6 cm

Sabina 1986.

Species	Chemical formula	Description
Mont Saint-Hilaire, Quebec		
actinolite	$Ca_2(Mg,Fe)_5Si_8O_{22}(OH)_2$	dark green to black; acicular; 5 mm
aegirine	$NaFeSi_2O_6$	green to black; long prismatic to acicular, radiating aggregates; 13 cm
albite	$NaAlSi_3O_8$	colourless, pale pink, white; tabular, platy, fine-grained massive; 3 cm
allanite	$(Ce,Ca,Y)_2(Al,Fe)_3(SiO_4)_3(OH)$	beige to dark brown; fibrous, acicular; 3 mm
analcime	$NaAlSi_2O_6 \cdot H_2O$	colourless, white, orange; trapezohedral, massive; 20 cm
anatase	TiO_2	black, dark blue; pyramidal, tabular; 3 mm
ancylite	$SrCe(CO_3)_2(OH) \cdot H_2O$	bluish gray to pink; prismatic; 5 mm
andradite	$Ca_3Fe_2(SiO_4)_3$	black to dark green; dodecahedral, trapezohedral, massive; 7 mm
anglesite	$PbSO_4$	apple-green, tan; equant, powdery; 1 mm
ankerite	$Ca(Fe,Mg,Mn)(CO_3)_2$	white; rhombohedral; 1 mm
annite	$KFe_3AlSi_3O_{10}(OH,F)_2$	dark green, black; short prismatic, micaceous; 2 cm
apatite group (*see* fluorapatite, carbonate-fluorapatite)		
apophyllite group (*see* fluorapophyllite, hydroxyapophyllite)		
aragonite	$CaCO_3$	colourless, white, pinkish-yellow; tabular to bladed; 4 mm
arfvedsonite	$Na_3(Fe,Mg)_4FeSi_8O_{22}(OH)_2$	black; long prismatic; 9 cm
arsenopyrite	$FeAsS$	silver-gray; short prismatic, flattened, striated, twinned, 5 mm
ashcroftine	$KNaCaY_2Si_6O_{12}(OH)_{10} \cdot 4H_2O$	pale pink; acicular, radiating aggregates; 5 mm
astrophyllite	$(K,Na)_3(Fe,Mn)_7Ti_2Si_8O_{24}(O,OH)_7$	bronze-yellow to red; bladed, lamellar; 4 cm
augite	$(Ca,Na)(Mg,Fe,Al,Ti)(Si,Al)_2O_6$	greenish brown; short prismatic; 2 mm
barite	$BaSO_4$	yellow; tabular; 3 mm
barylite	$BaBe_2Si_2O_7$	colourless; thin blades; 1 mm
barytolamprophyllite	$(Na,K)_2(Ba,Ca,Sr)_2(Ti,Fe)_3(SiO_4)_4(O,OH)_2$	pale to brownish yellow; fibrous to foliated blades; zoned with lamprophyllite; 12 mm
bastnaesite	$(Ce,La)(CO_3)F$	creamy white; pale blue, yellow to orange, olive green; acicular, radiating, platy, rosettes, prismatic, massive; 2 mm
bavenite	$Ca_4Be_2Al_2Si_9O_{26}(OH)_2$	colourless to beige; transparent, radiating aggregates of platy crystals; 5 mm

Species	Chemical formula	Description
behoite	$Be(OH)_2$	colourless to white; radiating spherical aggregates of spear-shaped prisms; 5 mm
berthierine	$(Fe,Mg)_{2\cdot3}(Si,Al)_2O_5(OH)_4$	gray to brown; pseudo-hexagonal prisms; 2 mm
beryl	$Be_3Al_2Si_6O_{18}$	pale green to yellowish green; prismatic; 0.5 mm
beudantite	$PbFe_3(AsO_4)(SO_4)(OH)_6$	yellow to olive-green; crystalline crusts and druses.
biotite	$K(Mg,Fe)_3(Al,Fe)Si_3O_{10}(OH,F)_2$	dark brown, black; prismatic, micaceous; 3 cm
birnessite	$Na_4Mn_{14}O_{27}\cdot9H_2O$	black; fine-grained coatings and replacements
bismuth	Bi	gray, metallic; irregular grains; 1 mm
britholite	$(Ce,Ca)_5(SiO_4,PO_4)_3(OH)F$	tan, dark brown; aggregates of fine needles, anhedral tabular; 1 cm
brockite	$(Ca,Th,Ce)(PO_4)\cdot H_2O$	white; powder
brookite	TiO_2	black; equant, striated prisms; 7 mm
burbankite	$(Na,Ca)_3(Sr,Ba,Ce)_3(CO_3)_5$	yellow to yellow-green; prismatic; 2 cm
calcioancylite	$(Ca,Sr)Ce(CO_3)_2(OH)\cdot H_2O$	colourless, pink; bladed; 0.5 mm
calcite	$CaCO_3$	colourless, white, yellow; tabular, rhombohedral, scalenohedral, botryoidal; 4 cm
cancrinite	$Na_6Ca_2Al_6Si_6O_{24}(CO_3)_2$	gray, purple, yellow; hexagonal prisms, massive; 4 cm
carbocernaite	$(Ca,Na)(Sr,Ce,Ba)(CO_3)_2$	yellow; irregular grains
carbonate-fluorapatite	$Ca_5(PO_4,CO_3)_3F$	honey-yellow to brown; botryoidal; 1 mm
carletonite	$KNa_4Ca_4Si_8O_{18}(CO_3)_4(OH,F)\cdot H_2O$	blue, pink; tetragonal prisms, cleavage masses; 4 cm
catapleiite	$Na_2ZrSi_3O_9\cdot2H_2O$	colourless, light brown, often iridescent; tabular to platy, rosettes; 5 cm (single crystals), 10 cm (rosettes)
celestine	$SrSO_4$	white to tan; compact spherical aggregates; 1 mm
cerite	$(Ce,Ca)_9(Mg,Fe)Si_7(O,OH,F)_{28}$	rose-red to pink; thin, transparent, hexagonal plates; 1 mm
cerussite	$PbCO_3$	white; powdery coating on galena
chabazite	$CaAl_2Si_4O_{12}\cdot6H_2O$	colourless; twinned, pseudo-hexagonal prisms; 0.1 mm
chalcopyrite	$CuFeS_2$	brassy yellow, metallic; pyramidal, massive; 1 mm (crystals), 1 cm (masses)

Species	Chemical formula	Description
chamosite	$(Fe,Mg)_5Al(Si_3Al)O_{10}(OH,O)_8$	dark brownish-green; spheres and micaceous plates; 15 mm
chkalovite	$Na_2BeSi_2O_6$	colourless; transparent, blocky; 1 mm
clinochlore	$(Mg,Fe)_5Al(Si_3Al)O_{10}(OH)_8$	brown, tan, colourless, white; tiny plates forming rosettes; 0.1 mm
cordylite	$Ba(Ce,La)_2(CO_3)_3F_2$	yellow, yellow-green, brown; prismatic (barrel-shaped); 13 mm
cryolite	Na_3AlF_6	colourless to white; octahedral-like; 2 mm
datolite	$CaBSiO_4(OH)$	pale yellow, white; short prismatic, compact spheres; 1 cm
dawsonite	$NaAl(CO_3)(OH)_2$	white to colourless; striated prisms, bladed cleavages; 2 cm
diopside	$CaMgSi_2O_6$	green; masses of tiny prisms in calcite; 1 mm
dolomite	$CaMg(CO_3)_2$	creamy white, yellowish; tabular, rhombohedral, botryoidal aggregates; 2 mm
donnayite	$Sr_3NaCaY(CO_3)_6 \cdot 3H_2O$	yellow, brown, white, gray; tabular, platy, barrel-shaped, saucer-shaped, rosettes; 2 mm
dorfmanite	$Na_2HPO_4 \cdot 2H_2O$	white; powder
doyleite	$Al(OH)_3$	colourless to white; plates, rosettes, globular; 0.5 mm
edingtonite	$BaAl_2Si_3O_{10} \cdot 4H_2O$	colourless; square prisms; 0.1 mm
elpidite	$Na_2ZrSi_6O_{15} \cdot 3H_2O$	grayish to creamy white; prismatic, acicular; 4 cm
epididymite	$NaBeSi_3O_7(OH)$	colourless, white; tabular, bladed, pseudo-hexagonal twins, acicular, reticulated; 15 mm
epidote	$Ca_2(Al,Fe)_3(SiO_4)_3(OH)$	dark brown to red brown; lustrous, tabular; 3 mm
epistolite	$Na_2(Nb,Ti)_2Si_2O_9 \cdot nH_2O$	beige, pink, yellow-gray, silky; platy, cleavage masses; 5 cm
eudialyte	$Na_4(Ca,Ce,Fe)_2ZrSi_6O_{17}(OH,Cl)_2$	brown, red, orange; rhombohedral, octahedral-like, short prismatic, massive; 3 cm
eudidymite	$NaBeSi_3O_7(OH)$	colourless, white, pale pink; tabular, stellate twins; 2 cm
ewaldite	$Ba(Ca,Y,Na,K)(CO_3)_2$	yellow; tabular, often interwoven with mckelveyite and donnayite; 2 mm
fluorapatite	$Ca_5(PO_4)_3F$	colourless, tan, yellowish; prismatic, fibrous, radiating aggregates; 4 mm
fluorapophyllite	$KCa_4Si_8O_{20}(F,OH) \cdot 8H_2O$	colourless, white, greenish yellow, pink; tabular to equant; 3 cm

Species	Chemical formula	Description
fluorite	CaF_2	colourless, yellowish green, pale blue, purple, pink; cleavages, cubic, octahedral, dodecahedral, often rounded; 17 cm
francolite	$Ca_5(PO_4,CO_3)_3F$	
franconite	$NaNb_3O_8 \cdot nH_2O$	white, silky; fibrous radiating aggregates; 0.1 mm
gaidonnayite	$Na_2ZrSi_3O_9 \cdot 2H_2O$	colourless, white, beige; tabular to equidimensional, spherical aggregates; 4 mm
galena	PbS	lead-gray, metallic; cubic, octahedral, 5 mm
ganophyllite	$(Na,K)(Mn,Fe,Al)_5$ $(Si,Al)_6O_{15}(OH)_5 \cdot 2H_2O$	yellow, brown; flat needles; 1 mm
garronite	$Na_2Ca_5Al_{12}Si_{20}O_{64}$ $\cdot 27H_2O$	grayish white, yellow, tan; prismatic, radiating aggregates; 0.2 mm
genthelvite	$Zn_4Be_3(SiO_4)_3S$	yellowish green, white; tetrahedral; 12 mm
gersdorffite	$NiAsS$	dull, dark gray; fine-grained intergrowths with calcite
gibbsite	$Al(OH)_3$	pink, white; radiating needles, powder; 0.2 mm
gismondine	$CaAl_2Si_2O_8 \cdot 4H_2O$	very pale pink to colourless, octahedral-like, 1 mm
gmelinite	$(Na_2,Ca)Al_2Si_4O_{12} \cdot 6H_2O$	yellow; tabular, spherical aggregates; 2 mm
goethite	$FeO(OH)$	dark brown, black; fine-grained aggregates
götzenite	$(Ca,Na)_3(Ti,Al)Si_2O_7$ $(F,OH)_2$	white; acicular; 4 mm
graphite	C	dark gray, fine-grained
greigite	Fe_3S_4	black; rounded grains; 1 mm
griceite	LiF	white to greenish yellow; compact, powdery botryoidal masses, cubic, stacked tapering aggregates of cubes; 1 mm
grossular	$Ca_3Al_2(SiO_4)_3$	medium brown; trapezohedral; 2 mm
gypsum	$CaSO_4 \cdot 2H_2O$	colourless, white; prismatic, bladed; 7 mm
halotrichite	$FeAl_2(SO_4)_4 \cdot 22H_2O$	white, silky; fibrous; 1 mm
harmotome	$(Ba,K)_{1-2}(Si,Al)_8$ $O_{16} \cdot 6H_2O$	colourless; twinned, square prisms; 0.3 mm
hedenbergite	$CaFeSi_2O_6$	pale yellow; transparent, radiating prisms; 3 mm
helvite	$Mn_4Be_3(SiO_4)_3S$	yellow; tetrahedral, massive; 5 mm
hematite	Fe_2O_3	dull red; fine-grained alteration

Species	Chemical formula	Description
hemimorphite	$Zn_4Si_2O_7(OH)_2 \cdot H_2O$	whitish gray; botryoidal; 0.2 mm
hilairite	$Na_2ZrSi_3O_9 \cdot 3H_2O$	light to dark brown; short prismatic; 4 mm
hochelagaite	$CaNb_4O_{11} \cdot nH_2O$	white; globular aggregates of radiating blades; 0.5 mm
hornblende	$Ca_2(Mg,Fe)_4Al(Si_7Al)$ $O_{22}(OH,F)_2$	brown, dark green, black; prismatic; 3 mm
hydrocerussite	$Pb_3(CO_3)_2(OH)_2$	white; crusts, tiny prisms on galena.
hydrogrossular	$Ca_3Al_2(SiO_4)_{3-x}(OH)_{4x}$	colourless; octahedral in stacked aggregates; 2 mm
hydrotalcite	$Mg_6Al_2(CO_3)$ $(OH)_{16} \cdot 4H_2O$	green, yellow; rounded plates, rhombohedral; 1 mm
hydroxyapophyllite	$KCa_4Si_8O_{20}(OH,F) \cdot 8H_2O$	colourless, white, greenish yellow, pink; tabular to equant; 3 cm
hydrozincite	$Zn_5(CO_3)_2(OH)_6$	white, grayish blue; porcelaneous crusts
ilmenite	$FeTiO_3$	black; thick tabular, platy; 2 cm
jarosite	$KFe_3(SO_4)_2(OH)_6$	yellow; powdery coatings.
joaquinite	$Ba_2NaCe_2Fe(Ti,Nb)_2$ $Si_8O_{26}(OH,F) \cdot H_2O$	yellow; bladed; 12 mm
kaersutite	$NaCa_2(Mg,Fe)_4Ti$ $(Si_6,Al_2)O_{22}(OH)_2$	black; prismatic phenocrysts; 4 cm
kainosite	$Ca_2(Y,Ce)_2Si_4O_{12}(CO_3) \cdot$ H_2O	pale brown; radiating aggregates of blades; 5 mm
kaolinite	$Al_2Si_2O_5(OH)_4$	white; powder
kupletskite	$(K,Na)_3(Mn,Fe)_7(Ti,Nb)_2$ $Si_8O_{24}(O,OH)_7$	bronze-yellow, slightly purple; bladed, lamellar; 3 mm
kutnohorite	$Ca(Mn,Mg,Fe)(CO_3)_2$	gray; equidimensional; 0.1 mm
labuntsovite	$(K,Ba,Na)(Ti,Nb)(Si,Al)_2$ $(O,OH)_7 \cdot H_2O$	red, orange; acicular, prismatic; 5 mm
lamprophyllite	$Na_2(Sr,Ba)_2Ti_3(SiO_4)_4$ $(OH,F)_2$	yellow, brown; tabular, acicular; zoned with barytolamprophyllite; 1 mm
lavenite	$(Na,Ca)_3ZrSi_2O_7$ $(O,OH,F)_2$	yellow; radiating aggregates of acicular crystals; 5 mm
leifite	$Na_2(Si,Al,Be)_7$ $(O,OH,F)_{14}$	white; striated hexagonal prisms, radiating fibres; 2 cm
lemoynite	$(Na,K)_2CaZr_2Si_{10}O_{26}$ $\cdot 5-6H_2O$	white to yellowish white; radiating aggregates of blades; 5 mm
lepidocrocite	$FeO(OH)$	brick-red; fine-grained, powdery
leucophanite	$(Na,Ca)_2BeSi_2(O,OH,F)_7$	yellow to green, white; tabular, equidimensional, rosettes; 2 cm
leucosphenite	$BaNa_4Ti_2B_2Si_{10}O_{30}$	pale blue to colourless; bladed; 1 cm

Species	Chemical formula	Description
lizardite	$Mg_3Si_2O_5(OH)_4$	green; fine-grained alteration
loellingite	$FeAs_2$	gray, metallic; prismatic; 6 mm
lorenzenite	$Na_2Ti_2Si_2O_9$	grayish brown; radiating fibres; 1 cm
lovozerite	$Na_2Ca(Zr,Ti)Si_6$ $(O,OH)_{18}$	brown; dodecahedral-like, twins; 1 mm
lueshite	$NaNbO_3$	black; pseudocubic; 0.5 mm
magadiite	$NaSi_7O_{13}(OH)_3 \cdot 4H_2O$	white; powder
magnesio-arfvedson- ite	$Na_3(Mg,Fe)_4FeSi_8O_{22}$ $(OH)_2$	black, bluish green; long prismatic; 9 cm
magnesite	$MgCO_3$	light grayish green; transparent, modified rhombohedra; 2 mm
magnetite	Fe_3O_4	black; octahedral, dodecahedral; 7 mm
manganneptunite	$KNa_2Li(Mn,Fe)_2Ti_2$ Si_8O_{24}	dark red, brown, orange; prismatic, equant; 3 cm
marcasite	FeS_2	brassy yellow, metallic; bladed, prismatic, netted; 3 mm
mckelveyite	$Ba_3Na(Ca,U)Y(CO_3)_6$ $\cdot 3H_2O$	yellow; stacked plates; 3 mm
microcline	$KAlSi_3O_8$	white, gray; blocky, tabular, prismatic, Baveno twins, cleavage masses; 30 cm
milarite	$K_2Ca_4Al_2Be_4Si_{24}O_{60} \cdot H_2O$	white; prismatic; 4 mm
mimetite	$Pb_5(A_5O_4)_3Cl$	white; acicular; 0.2 mm
miserite	$K(Ca,Ce)_4Si_5O_{13}(OH)$	raspberry-red; prismatic, granular; 5 mm
molybdenite-2H	MoS_2	lead-gray; platy, fine-grained; 3 mm
molybdenite-3R	MoS_2	lead-gray; platy, fine-grained, cylindrical; 3 mm
monazite	$(Ce,La,Nd,Th)PO_4$	tan, brown; tabular; 15 mm
monteregianite	$(Na,K)_6(Y,Ca)_2Si_{16}$ $O_{38} \cdot 10H_2O$	colourless, white, gray, mauve; prismatic, acicular, tabular; 2 cm
montmorillonite	$(Na,Ca)_{0.33}(Al,Mg)_2Si_4$ $O_{10}(OH)_2 \cdot nH_2O$	white; powder
mosandrite	$(Na,Ca,Ce)_3Ti(SiO_4)_2F$	brown; acicular; 15 mm
muscovite	$KAl_2(Si_3Al)O_{10}(OH, F)_2$	white; fine-grained, micaceous; 1 mm
nahpoite	Na_2HPO_4	white; powder
narsarsukite	$Na_2(Ti,Fe)Si_4(O,F)_{11}$	yellow, green, brown; tabular, short prismatic, equant; 15 mm
natrolite	$Na_2Al_2Si_3O_{10} \cdot 2H_2O$	colourless, white, pale beige, pink; prismatic, fibrous; 10 cm
natron	$Na_2CO_3 \cdot 10H_2O$	colourless; transparent masses; reverts rapidly to white thermonatrite; 4 cm

Species	Chemical formula	Description
natrophosphate	$Na_7(PO_4)_2F \cdot 19H_2O$	colourless, white; modified dodecahedral; 1 mm
neighborite	$NaMgF_3$	orange-brown; octahedral-like, cubo-octahedral-like; 0.5 mm
nenadkevichite	$(Na,Ca,K)(Nb,Ti)Si_2O_6$ $(O,OH) \cdot 2H_2O$	light brown, pink; tabular, prismatic, equidimensional; 3 mm
nepheline	$(Na,K)AlSiO_4$	gray; hexagonal prisms, massive; 15 mm
nordstrandite	$Al(OH)_3$	colourless, white, pink, beige; tabular, botryoidal aggregates; 1 mm
parakeldyshite	$Na_2ZrSi_2O_7$	colourless; irregular grains; 0.1 mm
paranatrolite	$Na_2Al_2Si_3O_{10} \cdot 3H_2O$	colourless; epitaxial overgrowths on natrolite, unstable in air, converts to tetranatrolite; 1 mm
paraumbite	$K_3Zr_2HSi_6O_{18} \cdot nH_2O$	gray; equidimensional; 0.5 mm
parisite	$(Ce,La)_2Ca(CO_3)_3F_2$	brownish yellow; tabular; 1 mm
pectolite	$NaCa_2Si_3O_8(OH)$	colourless, white; prismatic, acicular, fibrous; 4 cm
petarasite	$Na_5Zr_2Si_6$ $O_{18}(Cl,OH) \cdot 2H_2O$	brownish yellow, light greenish yellow; prismatic; 5 cm
phillipsite	$(K,Na,Ca)_{1-2}(Si,Al)_8$ $O_{16} \cdot 6H_2O$	colourless; prismatic, twinned; 2 mm
phlogopite	$KMg_3Si_3AlO_{10}(F,OH)_2$	brown; tabular, micaceous; 1 cm
polylithionite	$KLi_2AlSi_4O_{10}(F,OH)_2$	colourless, light brown; micaceous, platy, rosettes, fine-grained massive; 3 cm
poudretteite	$KNa_2B_3Si_{12}O_{30}$	colourless, pale pink; transparent, deeply etched, roughly hexagonal, barrel-shaped; 5 mm
prehnite	$Ca_2Al_2Si_3O_{10}(OH)_2$	pale green or gray; compact radiating aggregates; 1 cm
pyrite	FeS_2	brassy yellow, metallic; cubic, cubo-octahedral, pyritohedral; 2 cm
pyrochlore	$(Na,Ca)_2Nb_2O_6(OH,F)$	brown, orange, yellow; octahedral; 0.2 mm
pyrophanite	$MnTiO_3$	reddish brown, red; plates, rosettes; 1 cm
pyrrhotite	$Fe_{1-x}S$	bronzy yellow, metallic; hexagonal plates, tabular; 15 mm
quartz	SiO_2	colourless, gray, brown, black; prismatic; 8 cm
raite	$Na_4Mn_3Si_8(O,OH)_{24}$ $\cdot 9H_2O$	reddish brown; yellow; acicular; 0.2 mm
rhabdophane	$(Ce,La)PO_4 \cdot H_2O$	pale yellow, brown; hexagonal prisms; botryoidal; 15 mm

Species	Chemical formula	Description
rhodochrosite	$MnCO_3$	red, reddish brown; rhombohedral, tabular, rosettes; 10 cm
richterite	$Na_2Ca(Mg,Fe)_5Si_8O_{22}(OH)_2$	colourless, light green; prismatic; 3 mm
riebeckite	$Na_2(Fe,Mg)_3Fe_2Si_8O_{22}(OH)_2$	grayish blue, silky; fibrous; 6 cm
rosenbuschite	$(Ca,Na)_3(Zr,Ti)Si_2O_8F$	light yellow-orange; acicular, radiating; 3 mm
rutile	TiO_2	black; short prismatic, twinned; 2 mm
sabinaite	$Na_9Zr_4Ti_2O_9(CO_3)_8$	colourless; tabular; 2 mm
sanidine	$(K,Na)AlSi_3O_8$	colourless, white, pale pink; blocky, tabular; 0.5 mm
scheelite	$CaWO_4$	colourless; equidimensional
senaite	$Pb(Ti,Fe,Mn)_{21}O_{38}$	black, submetallic; equidimensional, twinned; 0.5 mm
sepiolite	$Mg_4Si_6O_{15}(OH)_2 \cdot 6H_2O$	white; fibrous, felt-like; 3 mm
serandite	$Na(Mn,Ca)_2Si_3O_8(OH)$	orange, pink; prismatic, bladed; 15 cm
siderite	$FeCO_3$	brown; rhombohedral, tabular, twinned; 25 cm
sodalite	$Na_8Al_6Si_6O_{24}Cl_2$	blue, gray, purple, white, yellowish; dodecahedral, massive; 3 cm
spessartine	$Mn_3Al_2(SiO_4)_3$	brown; rounded crystals; 5.5 cm
sphalerite	$(Zn,Fe)S$	black, brown, green, yellow; octahedral-like, tetrahedral, twinned, massive; 6 cm
steacyite	$Th(Ca,Na)_2K_{1-x}Si_8O_{20}$	brown, cream-white; tetragonal prisms; twinned; 2 mm
steenstrupine	$(Ce,La,Na,Mn)_6(Si,P)_6O_{18}(OH)$	black; massive; 2 mm
stillwellite	$(Ce,La,Ca)BSiO_5$	pale pink; hexagonal prisms, rhombohedral termination; 0.2 mm
strontianite	$SrCO_3$	colourless, white; bladed, acicular, radiating; 3 mm
synchisite	$(Ce,La)Ca(CO_3)_2F$	brown, gray; tabular; 15 mm
szomolnokite	$FeSO_4 \cdot H_2O$	white to yellow-stained; powdery
tadzhikite	$Ca_3(Ce,Y)_2(Ti,Al,Fe)B_4Si_4O_{22}$	pale yellow, yellowish brown; platy, sheaf-like aggregates; 0.2 mm
taeniolite	$KLiMg_2Si_4O_{10}F_2$	grayish brown; tapering, hexagonal prisms; 1 cm
terskite	$Na_4ZrSi_6O_{15} \cdot H_2O$	white; powdery to porcelaneous replacement of lovozerite

Species	Chemical formula	Description
tetrahedrite	$(Cu,Fe)_{12}Sb_4S_{13}$	black; fine-grained; 0.2 mm
tetranatrolite	$Na_2Al_2Si_3O_{10}\cdot2H_2O$	white; fine-grained coatings on natrolite
thalcusite	$Tl_2(Cu,Fe)_4S_4$	bronzy black; bladed; 1 mm
thaumasite	$Ca_3Si(CO_3)(SO_4)$ $(OH)_6\cdot12H_2O$	colourless, white; acicular, radiating; 2 mm
thermonatrite	$Na_2CO_3\cdot H_2O$	white; powder
thomsonite	$NaCa_2Al_5Si_5O_{20}\cdot6H_2O$	white, colourless; fibrous, compact spheres; 2 mm
thornasite	$(Na,K)ThSi_{11}(O,H_2,F,$ $Cl)_{33}$	colourless, fluoresces bright green (short wave); grains; 0.7 mm
thorogummite	$Th(SiO_4)_{1-x}(OH)_{4x}$	yellowish brown to red, resinous; masses; 0.5 mm
titanite	$CaTiSiO_5$	yellow, light brown; prismatic; 2 mm
trona	$Na_3(CO_3)(HCO_3)\cdot2H_2O$	white; powder
tundrite	$Na_3(Ce,La)_4(Ti,Nb)_2$ $(SiO_4)_2(CO_3)_3O_4(OH)$ $\cdot2H_2O$	yellow, greenish yellow; acicular, bladed; 3 cm
ussingite	$Na_2AlSi_3O_8(OH)$	pale pink, colourless; stacked, tabular; 2 mm
vesuvianite	$Ca_{10}Mg_2Al_4(SiO_4)_5$ $(Si_2O_7)_2(OH)_4$	dark to light green, yellow, brown; tetragonal prisms, acicular, fibrous radiating, 15 mm
villiaumite	NaF	pink, red; cubic, cubo-octahedral, cleavage masses; 5 cm
vinogradovite	$(Na,Ca,K)_4Ti_4AlSi_6O_{23}$ $(OH)\cdot2H_2O$	white; acicular, bladed, platy, radiating; 4 mm
vitusite	$Na_3(Ce,La,Nd)(PO_4)_2$	pinkish tan, black; poorly defined radiating prisms; 5 mm
vuonnemite	$Na_4TiNb_2Si_4O_{17}\cdot2Na_3$ PO_4	yellow; platy; 4 mm
willemite	Zn_2SiO_4	blue, gray; hexagonal prisms; 8 cm
woehlerite	$NaCa_2(Zr,Nb)Si_2O_8$ (O,OH,F)	yellow; prismatic, tabular; 5 mm
wollastonite	$CaSiO_3$	white; granular; 4 mm
wulfenite	$PbMoO_4$	yellow; acicular; 0.2 mm
wurtzite-2H	$(Zn,Fe)S$	red, tan; pyramidal, fine-grained replacement; 1 mm
wurtzite-4H	$(Zn,Fe)S$	dull apple-green, etched skeletal hexagonal prisms; 3 mm
xenotime	YPO_4	colourless, grayish white; tabular; 0.1 mm
yofortierite	$(Mn,Mg)_5Si_8O_{20}(OH)_2$ $\cdot8-9H_2O$	pink, violet; radiating matted fibres; 3 cm

Species	Chemical formula	Description
zeophyllite	$Ca_4Si_3O_8(OH,F)_4 \cdot 2H_2O$	white, silky; 1 mm
zircon	$ZrSiO_4$	brown, yellow; dipyramidal, prismatic; 2 cm

Chao 1971, 1855-66; Chao 1978, 561-5; Chao 1980, 85-8; Chao et al. 1974a, 237-40; Chao et al. 1974b, 316-19; Chao et al. 1978, 335-40; Chao et al. 1980, 497-502; Chao et al. 1985, 21-8; Chen, Chao 1980, 77-84; Grice et al. 1987, 763-766; Mandarino et al. 1988; Marble, Regis 1979, 4-25; Perrault, Szymanski 1982, 59-63; Perrault et al. 1969, 585-96; Perrault et al. 1975, 68-74; Wight, Chao 1986, 182-97.

Species	Chemical formula	Description
Francon Quarry, Montreal, Quebec		
aegirine	$NaFeSi_2O_6$	green, brown; acicular; 1 mm
albite	$NaAlSi_3O_8$	colourless, white; platy; 2 mm
almandine	$Fe_3Al_2(SiO_4)_3$	pink; massive
analcime	$NaAlSi_2O_6 \cdot H_2O$	colourless, white, green, yellow, orange, brown; trapezohedral, cubic; fine-grained; 5 mm
anatase	TiO_2	gray, sub-metallic; flaky aggregates
ankerite	$Ca(Fe,Mg,Mn)(CO_3)_2$	white, yellow; aggregates of rhombohedra; 1 mm
apatite group	$Ca_5(PO_4)_3(F,Cl,OH)$	gray; fine-grained
baddeleyite	ZrO_2	tan, yellow; fine-grained powder
barite	$BaSO_4$	colourless, white, gray, yellow, pink; tabular, bladed, rosettes, fine-grained; 2 cm
brookite	TiO_2	black; platy rosettes, fine-grained
calcite	$CaCO_3$	colourless, white, gray, yellow; scalenohedral, rhombohedral, blocky, cone-shaped, spear-shaped, 15 mm
celestite	$SrSO_4$	blue, yellow, pink, colourless; prismatic, bladed, acicular; 8 mm
chromite	$FeCr_2O_4$	black; grains
cristobalite	SiO_2	white, bluish; botryoidal, matted fibres; 3 mm
crocoite	$PbCrO_4$	yellow, waxy; massive
cryolite	Na_3AlF_6	colourless, yellow; octahedral-like; 1 cm
dachiardite	$(Ca,Na_2,K_2)_5Al_{10}Si_{38}O_{96} \cdot 25H_2O$	white, silky; fibrous, acicular, radiating; 2 mm
dawsonite	$NaAl(CO_3)(OH)_2$	colourless, white; striated prisms, acicular, fibrous spheres, waxy, flaky; 8 mm
dolomite	$CaMg(CO_3)_2$	colourless, white, yellow, pink, green; rhombohedral, granular; 1 mm
doyleite	$Al(OH)_3$	white; fine-grained crusts, botryoidal
dresserite	$BaAl_2(CO_3)_2(OH)_4 \cdot H_2O$	white, silky; fibrous, spherical aggregates; 1 mm
elpidite	$Na_2ZrSi_6O_{15} \cdot 3H_2O$	colourless, white; fibrous, acicular; 2 mm
fluorite	CaF_2	colourless, white, pink, purple, brown, green; cubic, sugary aggregates; 3 mm
franconite	$(Na,Ca)_2(Nb,Ti)_4O_{11} \cdot nH_2O$	white; globules; 0.1 mm
galena	PbS	lead-gray, metallic; octahedral, cubic; 5 mm

Species	Chemical formula	Description
glauconite	$(K,Na)(Fe,Al,Mg)_2$ $(Si,Al)_4O_{10}(OH)_2$	gray; clay-like coatings
goethite	$FeO(OH)$	yellow, brown; fibrous, flaky, rosettes, earthy
graphite	C	black; flaky aggregates
gypsum	$CaSO_4 \cdot 2H_2O$	colourless; platy, tabular, acicular; 5 cm
halite	$NaCl$	white; fine-grained patches
halloysite	$Al_2Si_2O_5(OH)_4$	white; powdery to compact masses
harmotome	$(Ba,K)_{1-2}(Si,Al)_8O_{16} \cdot 6H_2O$	gray; fine-grained crusts
hematite	Fe_2O_3	reddish brown, black; fine-grained botryoidal crusts
hochelagaite	$CaNb_4O_{11} \cdot nH_2O$	white; globular aggregates of radiating blades; 0.5 mm
humboldtine	$FeC_2O_4 \cdot 2H_2O$	yellow; botryoidal aggregates; 1 mm
"hydrocarbon"		brown, black; irregular films and crusts
hydrocerussite	$Pb_3(CO_3)_2(OH)_2$	gray, white; powdery coating on galena
hydrodresserite	$BaAl_2(CO_3)_2(OH)_4 \cdot 3H_2O$	white; fibrous, spherical aggregates; 1 mm
ilmenorutile	$(Ti,Nb,Fe)_3O_6$	black; platy; 1 mm
kaolinite	$Al_2Si_2O_5(OH)_4$	white; flaky aggregates
magnetite	Fe_3O_4	black; massive
marcasite	FeS_2	brassy yellow, metallic, tarnished; bladed, rosettes, cyclic twins; 5 mm
molybdenite	MoS_2	lead-gray, metallic; flakes
montmorillonite	$(Na,Ca)_{0.33}(Al,Mg)_2Si_4$ $O_{10}(OH_2 \cdot nH_2O$	white, gray; flaky, fibrous spherical aggregates
montroyalite	$Sr_4Al_8(CO_3)_3(OH,F)_{26}$ $\cdot 10\text{-}11\ H_2O$	white; radiating fibres forming balls; 1 mm
mordenite	$(Ca,Na_2,K_2)Al_2Si_{10}O_{24}$ $\cdot 7H_2O$	white; matted fibrous aggregates
nahcolite	$NaHCO_3$	white; fibrous, earthy aggregates, rosettes
natrojarosite	$NaFe_3(SO_4)_2(OH)_6$	yellow; powdery, scaly crusts
pseudorutile	$Fe_2Ti_3O_9$	black; fine-grained
pyrite	FeS_2	brassy yellow, metallic; cubes, modified cubes, spherical aggregates; 2 mm
pyrochlore	$(Na,Ca)_2Nb_2O_6(OH,F)$	orange; fine-grained
pyrrhotite	$Fe_{1-x}S$	bronze, metallic; flakes
quartz	SiO_2	colourless, white, smoky; prismatic, stacked sub-parallel aggregates, fine-grained massive; 4 cm

Species	Chemical formula	Description
rozenite	$FeSO_4 \cdot 4H_2O$	white; powder
rutile	TiO_2	black; minute plates; 1 mm
sabinaite	$Na_9Zr_4Ti_2O_9(CO_3)_8$	white; powdery, chalky coatings
siderite	$FeCO_3$	amber, greenish; aggregates of rhombohedra; 1 mm
smythite	$(Fe,Ni)_9S_{11}$	brown, black, metallic; flakes, plates, rosettes; 0.5 mm
sodium dachiardite	$(Na_2,Ca,K_2)_{4\text{-}5}Al_8Si_{40}O_9 \cdot 26H_2O$	white; fibrous, acicular, radiating; 2 mm
sphalerite	$(Zn,Fe)S$	yellow, amber, orange; complex, rounded, twins, botryoidal; 1 mm
strontianite	$SrCO_3$	colourless, white, amber, green, yellow, pink; bladed, acicular, radiating fibrous, spheres; 1 cm
strontio-dresserite	$(Sr,Ca)Al_2(CO_3)_2(OH)_4 \cdot H_2O$	white, silky; radiating blades forming spheres, crusts; 0.1 mm
sulphur	S	creamy white, black; earthy aggregates admixed with pyrite and sphalerite
synchisite	$(Ce,La)Ca(CO_3)_2F$	white, brown, silky; fibrous, platy, spherical, powdery aggregates
thenardite	Na_2SO_4	white; powdery crusts
thorbastnaesite	$Th(Ca,Ce)(CO_3)_2F_2 \cdot 3H_2O$	white; fibrous spherical aggregates, crusts; 0.5 mm
viitaniemiite	$Na(Ca,Mn)Al(PO_4)(F,OH)_3$	colourless; bladed, radiating; 2 mm
weloganite	$Sr_3Na_2Zr(CO_3)_6 \cdot 3H_2O$	yellow, green, gray, colourless; deeply striated hexagonal-shaped prisms, stacked plates; 6 cm
zircon	$ZrSiO_4$	pink, yellow, brown, gray; fine-grained

Bonardi et al. 1981, 285-9; Chao et al. 1985, 21-8; Jambor et al. 1969, 84-9; Jambor et al. 1977a, 399-404; Jambor et al. 1977b, 405-7; Jambor et al. 1980, 25-9; Jambor et al. 1984, 239-43; Jambor et al. 1986, 449-53; Ramik et al. 1983, 499-502; Roberts et al. 1986, 455-9; Sabina 1979, 115-20; Sabina et al. 1968, 468-77.

Species	Chemical formula	Description
Jeffrey Mine, Asbestos, Quebec		
actinolite	$Ca_2(Mg,Fe)_5Si_8O_{22}(OH)_2$	white; coarse fibrous, splintery; 30 cm
albite	$NaAlSi_3O_8$	colourless, white; tabular; 2 cm
allanite	$(Ce,Ca,Y)_2(Al,Fe)_3$ $(SiO_4)_3(OH)$	brown-black, platy; 1 mm
andalusite	Al_2SiO_5	lavender; aggregates of elongated prisms; 15 cm
andradite	$Ca_3Fe_2(SiO_4)_3$	green; dodecahedral, trapezohedral; 5 mm
antigorite	$(Mg,Fe)_3Si_2O_5(OH)_4$	green; compact fibrous, splintery; 60 cm
apophyllite	$(K,Na)Ca_4Si_8O_{20}(F,OH)$ $\cdot 8H_2O$	colourless; blocky; 4 cm
aragonite	$CaCO_3$	white, pale yellow; acicular, globular; 1 cm
artinite	$Mg_2(CO_3)(OH)_2 \cdot 3H_2O$	white; fibrous, radiating; 5 mm
biotite	$K(Mg,Fe)_3(Al,Fe)Si_3O_{10}$ $(OH,F)_2$	black; hexagonal-shaped plates; micaceous; 10 cm
brucite	$Mg(OH)_2$	pale green; fine-grained massive, fibrous; 160 cm
calcite	$CaCO_3$	white; rhombohedral; botryoidal, columnar; 15 cm
celestite	$SrSO_4$	white; earthy
chalcocite	Cu_2S	black, metallic; anhedral blebs; 3 mm
chlorite	$(Al,Fe,Li,Mg,Mn,Ni)_{5-6}$ $(Al,B,Fe,Si)_4O_{10}(OH)_8$	green; hexagonal plates; 5 mm
chromite	$FeCr_2O_4$	black; irregular blebs; 1 mm
chrysotile	$Mg_3Si_2O_5(OH)_4$	pale green; fibrous; 5 cm
clinochlore	$(Mg,Fe)_5Al(Si_3Al)O_{10}$ $(OH)_8$	grayish green; platy, micaceous; 25 mm
clinozoisite	$Ca_2Al_3(SiO_4)_3(OH)$	colourless, mauve; prismatic; 15 mm
copper	Cu	dark brown, metallic; flakes; 0.5 mm
cubanite	$CuFe_2S_3$	bronzy yellow; massive, anhedral, platy; 5 mm
cuprite	Cu_2O	red; fine-grained coating
diaspore	$AlO(OH)$	lavender; cleavage masses; 2 cm
diopside	$CaMgSi_2O_6$	white, lavender, green; prismatic, bladed; 3 cm
dolomite	$CaMg(CO_3)_2$	pink; botryoidal; 1 mm
galena	PbS	lead-gray, metallic; anhedral grains; 3 mm
grossular	$Ca_3Al_2(SiO_4)_3$	colourless, white, pink, orange, green; trapezohedral; dodecahedral; 3 cm
groutite	$MnO(OH)$	black; radiating, fibrous; 3 mm
heazlewoodite	Ni_3S_2	bronze, metallic; subhedral grains, rhombohedral; 4 mm

Species	Chemical formula	Description
"hydrocarbon"		brown-black; blebs; 6 cm
hydromagnesite	$Mg_5(CO_3)_4(OH)_2\cdot4H_2O$	white; platy, radiating, globular; 1 mm
hydrotalcite	$Mg_6Al_2(CO_3)(OH)_{16}$ $\cdot4H_2O$	white; hexagonal plates; 0.5 mm
jeffreyite	$(Ca,Na)_2(Be,Al)Si_2$ $(O,OH)_7$	clear, colourless; platy; 1.2 mm
lizardite	$Mg_3Si_2O_5(OH)_4$	white; massive, fine-grained
loellingite	$FeAs_2$	silver-white, metallic; platy; 4 mm
magnetite	Fe_3O_4	black, metallic; irregular blebs, columnar; 10 cm
manganite	$MnO(OH)$	black, prismatic; 7 mm
maucherite	$Ni_{11}As_8$	tin-white; irregular blebs; 0.1 mm
microcline	$KAlSi_3O_8$	white; cleavage masses; 6 cm
molybdenite	MoS_2	lead-gray, metallic; massive, fine-grained
muscovite	$KAl_2(Si_3Al)O_{10}(OH,F)_2$	colourless, light green; platy, micaceous; 3 cm
nickeline	$NiAs$	bronze, metallic; anhedral blebs; 0.25 mm
nickel-iron	(Fe,Ni)	silver-white, metallic; granular; 0.1 mm
okenite	$CaSi_2O_4(OH)_2\cdot H_2O$	white; fibrous, radiating; 8 mm
palygorskite	$(Mg,Al)_2Si_4O_{10}$ $(OH)\cdot4H_2O$	gray; fibrous, parchment-like sheets; 20 cm
paratacamite	$Cu_2(OH)_3Cl$	green; botryoidal; 0.5 mm
pectolite	$NaCa_2Si_3O_8(OH)$	white, gray; prismatic, fibrous; 2 cm
phlogopite	$KMg_3Si_3AlO_{10}(F,OH)_2$	dark brown; elongate hexagonal-shaped prisms, micaceous; 10 cm
prehnite	$Ca_2Al_2Si_3O_{10}(OH)_2$	colourless, white, pale yellow, green, purple; steep pyramidal, blocky, curved aggregates; 7 cm
pumpellyite	$Ca_2MgAl_2(SiO_4)(Si_2O_7)$ $(OH)_2\cdot H_2O$	pale green; acicular; 1 cm
pyroaurite	$Mg_6Fe_2(CO_3)(OH)_{16}$ $\cdot4H_2O$	amber; tabular; 0.5 mm
pyrochroite	$Mn(OH)_2$	orange-yellow; scaly
pyrrhotite	$Fe_{1-x}S$	bronzy yellow; irregular blebs; 1 cm
quartz	SiO_2	colourless, white; prismatic; 5 cm
schorl	$NaFe_3Al_6(BO_3)_3Si_6O_{18}$ $(OH)_4$	black; prismatic, divergent; 7 cm
spertiniite	$Cu(OH)_2$	blue; botryoidal; 0.1 mm
sphalerite	$(Zn,Fe)S$	brown; irregular blebs; 2 cm

Species	Chemical formula	Description
tacharanite	$Ca_{12}Al_2Si_{18}O_{51} \cdot 18H_2O$	white; botryoidal, powdery coatings
thomsonite	$NaCa_2Al_5Si_5O_{20} \cdot 6H_2O$	white; radiating, acicular, stellate; 2 cm
tochilinite	$6Fe_{0.9}S \cdot 5(Mg,Fe)(OH)_2$	bronzy black; soft, lamellar masses; 25 cm
vesuvianite	$Ca_{10}Mg_2Al_4(SiO_4)_5$ $(Si_2O_7)_2(OH)_4$	brown, green, purple; prismatic; 2 cm
wollastonite	$CaSiO_3$	colourless, white; fine-grained massive, fibrous, prismatic; 12 cm
xonotlite	$Ca_6Si_6O_{17}(OH)_2$	white; fine-grained massive, fibrous, splintery; 10 cm
zoisite	$Ca_2Al_3(SiO_4)_3(OH)$	pink; elongate plates, radiating; 15 mm

Grice, Williams 1979, 69-80; Grice, Gasparrini 1981, 337-40; Grice, Robinson 1984, 443-6.

Lake Harbour Area, Baffin Island, Northwest Territories

almandine	$Fe_3Al_2(SiO_4)_3$	red; trapezohedral; 2 cm
calcite	$CaCO_3$	white; cleavages; 10 cm
clinohumite	$(Mg,Fe)_9(SiO_4)_4(F,OH)_2$	yellow; irregular blebs; 1 cm
diopside	$CaMgSi_2O_6$	green; prismatic; 10 cm
forsterite	Mg_2SiO_4	yellowish brown; tabular; 2 cm
graphite	C	steel-gray; hexagonal plates, foliated, columnar, flakes; 5 cm
hornblende	$Ca_2(Mg,Fe)_4Al(Si_7Al)$ $O_{22}(OH,F)_2$	brown, green; stubby prismatic; 3 cm
lazurite	$(Na,Ca)_{7\text{-}8}(Al,Si)_{12}(O,S)_{24}$ $[(SO_4),Cl_2,(OH)_2]$	blue, pale green; massive, irregular grains; 5 mm
meionite	$3CaAl_2Si_2O_8 \cdot CaCO_3$	colourless, white, pale pink; stubby prismatic, massive; 15 mm
oligoclase	$(Na,Ca)Al(Al,Si)Si_2O_8$	white, pale blue; stubby prismatic, cleavage masses, twinning; 40 cm
phlogopite	$KMg_3Si_3AlO_{10}(F,OH)_2$	light amber, black; pseudohexagonal tapering prisms, cleavage masses, micaceous; 45 cm
quartz	SiO_2	white, smoky; rounded prisms, irregular blebs; 5 cm
spinel	$MgAl_2O_4$	purple; octahedral; 3 cm
titanite	$CaTiSiO_5$	yellowish green, black; wedge-shaped; 13 cm
uvite	$(Ca,Na)(Mg,Fe)_3Al_5Mg$ $(BO_3)_3Si_6O_{18}(OH,F)_4$	reddish brown; irregular grains; 3 cm

Grice, Gault 1983, 12-19.

Species	Chemical formula	Description
Nain, Labrador		
augite	$(Ca,Na)(Mg,Fe,Al,Ti)(Si,Al)_2O_6$	black; cleavage masses; 30 cm
hypersthene	$(Mg,Fe)_2Si_2O_6$	dark brown, bronze schiller; cleavage masses, lamellar twinning; 15 cm
labradorite	$(Ca,Na)Al(Al,Si)Si_2O_8$	dark gray, play of colours — blue, green, red, yellow, pink; cleavage masses, twinning; 30 cm

Emslie et al. 1972

Species	Chemical formula	Description
Bay of Fundy, Nova Scotia		
analcime	$NaAlSi_2O_6 \cdot H_2O$	white, colourless; trapezohedral; 7 cm
apophyllite	$(K,Na)Ca_4Si_8O_{20}(F,OH)\cdot 8H_2O$	white, colourless, light green; cubic-like, thick tabular; 5 cm
calcite	$CaCO_3$	colourless, honey-yellow; rhombohedral, scalenohedral; 5 cm
chabazite	$CaAl_2Si_4O_{12} \cdot 6H_2O$	colourless, white, reddish brown, greenish; rhombohedral, lenticular, twinned; 3 cm
copper	Cu	red, brown, metallic; irregular blebs, thin sheets; 4 cm
epistilbite	$CaAl_2Si_6O_{16} \cdot 5H_2O$	colourless, white; radiating fibres
gmelinite	$(Na_2,Ca)Al_2Si_4O_{12} \cdot 6H_2O$	light tan; short hexagonal prisms, lenticular, twinned; 1 cm
gypsum	$CaSO_4 \cdot 2H_2O$	colourless, white, pink, orange; fibrous aggregates, fine-grained massive, cleavages; 15 cm
gyrolite	$Ca_2Si_3O_7(OH)_2 \cdot H_2O$	white; concentric radiating plates; 3 mm
heulandite	$(Na,Ca)_{2\text{-}3}Al_3(Al,Si)_2Si_{13}O_{36} \cdot 12H_2O$	colourless, white, beige, pearly; trapezoidal, curved tabular aggregates; 2 cm
laumontite	$CaAl_2Si_4O_{12} \cdot 4H_2O$	white; radiating, prismatic; 15 mm
mesolite	$Na_2Ca_2Al_6Si_9O_{30} \cdot 8H_2O$	colourless, white; radiating acicular, prismatic; 10 cm
montmorillonite	$(Na,Ca)_{0.33}(Al,Mg)_2Si_4O_{10}(OH)_2 \cdot nH_2O$	pale yellow; radiating compact fibres; 5 mm
mordenite	$(Ca,Na_2,K_2)Al_2Si_{10}O_{24} \cdot 7H_2O$	white, slightly beige, pink; compact fibres
natrolite	$Na_2Al_2Si_3O_{10} \cdot 2H_2O$	colourless, white; fibrous, acicular; 2 cm
quartz	SiO_2	colourless, white, purple (amethyst); short prismatic, pyramidal; 3 cm

Species	Chemical formula	Description
quartz, chalcedony	SiO_2	white; yellow, red, brown (jasper); blue, gray, pink, orange, red (agate); fine-grained
scolecite	$CaAl_2Si_3O_{10} \cdot 3H_2O$	white; radiating, acicular; 12 cm
stilbite	$NaCa_2Al_5Si_{13}O_{36} \cdot 14H_2O$	white, orange, pink, red; bladed, radiating, sheaf-like aggregates; 6 cm
thomsonite	$NaCa_2Al_5Si_5O_{20} \cdot 6H_2O$	white; bladed, radiating; 3 mm

Sabina 1964.

Bibliography

Selected Reading

Armstrong, G.H. 1930. The Origin and
Meaning of Place Names in Canada.
Macmillan of Canada, Toronto.

Beiser, A. 1980. The Earth. *In* Life Nature
Library. Time-Life Books, New York.

Book of Minerals, by Albertus Magnus. n.d.
Trans. D. Wickoff. Clarendon Press,
Oxford, 1967.

Bruemmer, F. 1974. The Arctic. Inforcor Ltd.,
Montreal.

Budge, Wallis, E.A. 1968. Amulets and
Talismans. University Books, New
Hyde Park, N.Y.

Dayton, J. 1978. Minerals, Metals, Glazing
and Man. George G. Harrap & Co.
Ltd., London, Eng.

De Re Metallica, by Georgius Agricola. Trans.
of 1556 edn by H.C. and L.H. Hoover.
Dover Publications Inc., New York,
1950.

Desautels, P.E. 1968. The Mineral Kingdom.
Grosset & Dunlop Inc., Italy & Canada.

Desautels, P.E. 1971. The Gem Kingdom.
Random House, New York.

Embrey, P.G. and Fuller, J.P. 1980. A
Manual of New Mineral Names
1892-1978. Oxford University Press,
New York.

Encyclopedia of Science and Technology.
1982. McGraw Hill, New York.

Hamilton, W.R., Woolley, A.R. and Bishop,
A.C. 1974. The Hamlyn Guide to
Minerals, Rocks and Fossils. The
Hamlyn Publishing Group, London,
New York, Sydney, Toronto.

Hewitt, D.F. 1964. Rocks and Minerals of
Ontario. Frank Fogg, Toronto.

Hurlbut, C.S. 1969. Minerals and Man.
Random House, New York.

Knauth, P. 1974. The Metalsmith. Time-Life
Books, New York.

Le Bourdais, D.M. 1957. Metals and Men: the
Story of Canadian Mining. McClelland
& Stewart, Toronto.

Leechman, D. 1962. Native Tribes of Canada.
W.J. Gage & Co. Ltd., Toronto.

Mitchell, R.S. 1979. Mineral Names, What Do
They Mean? Van Nostrand Reinhold
Co., New York & Toronto.

Mowat, Farley. 1967. Canada North,
McClelland & Stewart Ltd., Toronto.

Pough, F.H. 1976. A Field Guide to Rocks
and Minerals. Houghton Mifflin
Company, Boston.

Putnam, D.F., Putnam, R.G. 1970. Canada: a
regional analysis. J.M. Dent & Sons
(Can) Ltd.

Ray, A.J. 1974. Indians in the Fur Trade.
Univ. of Toronto Press, Toronto.

Reader's Digest Association of Canada Ltd.
1968. Canada: This Land, These People.
Canada.

Sabina, A.F. 1963. Rocks and Minerals for
The Collector: Sudbury to Winnipeg.
Queen's Printer, Ottawa.

Sabina, A.F. 1964. Rock and Mineral Collecting in Canada. Queen's Printer, Ottawa.

Sorrell, C.A. 1973. A Field Guide and Introduction to the Geology and Chemistry of Rocks and Minerals. Golden Press, New York.

Tart, H. 1976. Jewellery Through 7,000 years. Rep. 78. British Museum Publs Ltd., London.

References

Chapter 1
Douglas, R.J.W. (ed.). 1969. Geology of Economic Minerals of Canada. Queen's Printer, Ottawa.

Chapter 2
Berton, P. 1969. The Klondike Fever. Alfred A. Knopf, New York.

Berton, P. 1972. Klondike — The Last Great Gold Rush. McClelland & Stewart, Toronto.

Berton, P. 1983. The Klondike Fever. McClelland & Stewart, Toronto.

Boillot, L. 1899. Aux Mines D'Or du Klondike du lac Bennett a Dawson City. Hachette et Co., Paris.

Boyle, R.W. 1979. The Geochemistry of Gold — Its Deposits, Energy, Mines & Resources, Minister of Supply & Services, Canada. Southern Murray, Toronto.

Hoffman, A. 1947. Free Gold. Associated Book Service, New York.

Luhrmann, W.B. 1969. The First Book of Gold, Franklin Watts Inc., New York.

Sutherland, C.H.V. 1969. Gold, Its Beauty, Power and Allure. McGraw-Hill, New York.

Chapter 3
Emmons, G.T. 1923. Jade in British Columbia and Alaska, and its Use by Natives. Museum of the American Indian, New York.

Jennes, D. 1963. The Indians of Canada. Roger Duhamel, Ottawa.

Leaming, S.F. 1978. Jade in Canada. GSC, Ottawa.

Niblack, A.P. 1973. Coast Indians of Southern Alaska and Northern B.C. Johnson Reprint Corp.

Smith, B., Wong, W. 1973. China: A History of Art. Harper & Row, New York.

Stewart, H. 1973. Artifacts of the Northwest Coast Indians. General Publishing Co. Ltd., Don Mills, Ont.

Zara, L. 1969. Jade. Walker & Co. New York.

Chapter 4
Cunynghame, F. 1953. Lost Trail. Faber & Faber Ltd., London.

Daniels, R. 1968. Alexander Mackenzie — the North West. Faber & Faber, London.

Franklin, J. 1971. Narrative of a Second Expedition to the Shores of the Polar Sea in the Years 1825, 1826, 1827. M.G. Hurtig Ltd., Edmonton.

Leslie, J.M. 1831. Discovery and Adventure on the Polar Seas & Regions. J & J Harper, New York.

Mackenzie, A. 1971. Voyages from Montreal on the River St Lawrence through the Continent of North America to the Frozen and Pacific Oceans, 1789-1793. M.G. Hurtig Ltd., Edmonton.

Moir, J.S., Saunders, R.E. 1970. Northern Destiny. J.M. Dent & Sons (Can) Ltd.

Chapter 6
Russell, D.A. 1977. A Vanished World. The Dinosaurs of Western Canada. NMNS, NMC, Ottawa.

Chapter 7
Archer, J.H. 1980. Saskatchewan, A History. Western Producer Prairie Books, Saskatoon, Saskatchewan.

Novacs, M.L. 1974. Esterhazy and Early Hungarian Immigration to Canada. Canadian Plains Studies, Regina, Saskatchewan.

Chapter 8
Elson, J.A. 1961. History of Glacial Lake Agassiz. Dept. of Geo. Sciences. McGill University Museum Publ., Montreal.

Last, W.M. 1984. Sedimentology of Playa Lakes of Northern Great Plains, Can. Journ. Earth Sciences.

Teller, J.T., Clayton, L. 1983. Glacial Lake Agassiz. Univ. of Toronto Press, Toronto.

Teller, J.T. (ed.). 1984. Natural Heritage of Manitoba. Legacy of the Ice Age. Manitoba Museum of Man and Nature, and Manitoba Nature Magazine.

Chapter 10
Gem and Mineral Federation of Canada. 1979. Rocks and Minerals in Canada. Consolidated Amethyst Communication Inc., Scarborough, Ont.

Chapter 11
Township of Michipicoten. 1979. Heritage, Michipicoten. Township of Michipicoten, Ont.

Turcott, A.W. 1967. Land of the Big Goose. Wawa Hist. Soc., Wawa, Ont.

Chapter 12
Baine, R.R. 1969. The Sudbury Region. Holt, Rinehart & Winston, Toronto.

Boldt, J.R. Jnr. 1967. The Winning of Nickel. Longman Canada Ltd., Toronto.

Burt, O.W. 1968. The First Book of Copper. Watts Inc., New York.

Howard-White, F.B. 1963. Nickel, an Historical Review. Longman Canada Ltd., Toronto.

Jones, R.L. 1972. Annotated Bibliography of Sudbury Area. Sudbury Publ. Libr., Sudbury, Ont.

Le Bourdais, D.M. 1957. Sudbury Basin: The Story of Nickel. Ryerson Press, Toronto.

St Amant, J.C. 1979. L'Industrie du nickel à Sudbury au debut du 22e siècle. Societé Historique du Nouvel-Ontario. Univ. of Sudbury, Ont.

Tracy, E.B. 1964. The New World of Copper. Dodd, Mead & Co., New York.

Chapter 13
Boldwin, D. 1978. Cobalt: a Pictorial History of the Development of Silver Mining. Highway Book Shop. Cobalt, Ontario.

Brown, Carson L. July, 1963. Cobalt — the town with the silver lining. Can. Geog. Journ.

Gibson, T.W. 1937. Mining in Ontario. T.E. Bowman, Toronto.

Groom, M. 1971. The Melted Years. Temiskaming Printing Co., New Liskeard, Ont.

Wright, J.V. 1972. Ontario Prehistory. NMC, Ottawa.

Wright, J.V. 1976. Six Chapters of Canada's Prehistory. NMC, Ottawa.

Chapter 14
Hewitt, D.F. 1969. Geology and Scenery — Peterborough, Bancroft and Madoc area. Ont. Dept. of Mines.

Hewitt, D.F., Freeman, E.B. 1972. Rocks and Minerals of Ontario. Ont. Dept. of Mines & Northern Affairs, Toronto.

Reynolds, N. 1979. Bancroft, A Bonanza of Memories. Bancroft Centennial Committee, Hillen Enterprises.

Satterley, J. 1957. Radioactive Mineral Occurrences in the Bancroft Area. Baptist Johnson, Toronto.

Sabina, A.P. 1986. Rocks and Minerals for the Collector: Bancroft-Parry Sound area and Southern Ontario. Queen's Printer. Ottawa.

Chapter 15
Creighton, D. 1956. The Empire of the St Lawrence. Macmillan of Canada, Toronto.

Moore, A.H. 1929. The Valley of the Richelieu. E.R. Smith Co. Ltd., St Johns, P.Q.

Wright, J.V. 1980. La Préhistoire du Québec. Musée nationaux du Canada, Montreal.

Chapter 17
Asbestos Manufacturers Co. Ltd. 1936. The Best in Asbestos. (Call. #McNf.A792). London.

Becker and Haag. 1928. Asbestos, Berlin, (GD.SC McNf.A79.F).

Sinclair, W.E. 1959. Asbestos, its Origin, Production and Utilization. Mining Publications Ltd., London.

Chapter 19
Mowat, C. 1983. The Outport People. McClelland & Stewart, Toronto.

Rowe, F.W. 1980. A History of Newfoundland and Labrador. McGraw-Hill, Ryerson Ltd., Toronto.

Tuck, J.A. 1976. Newfoundland and Labrador Prehistory. Van Nostrand Reinhold Ltd., Toronto.

Whitely, G. 1982. Northern Seas, Hardy Sailors. W.W. Norton & Co., New York.

Chapter 20

Hudgons, A.D. 1960. The Geology of the Northern Mountain on the Map Area, Baxters Harbour to Victoria Beach. M.Sc., thesis, Acadia Univ. Wolfville, Nova Scotia.

Appendix 3

Bonardi, M., Roberts, A.C. & Sabina, A.P. 1981. Sodium-rich dachiardite from the Francon quarry, Montreal Island, Quebec. Can. Mineral. 19.

Cabri, L.J. & Laflamme, J.H.G. 1976. The mineralogy of the platinum-group elements from some copper-nickel deposits of the Sudbury area, Ontario. Econ. Geol. 71.

Cerny, P. 1982. The Tanco pegmatite at Bernic Lake, southeastern Manitoba. Mineral. Assoc. Can. short course handbook 8.

Chao, G.Y. 1971. Carletonite, $KNa_4CA_4Si_8O_8(CO_3)^4$ (F,OH) H_2O, a new mineral from Mont St-Hilaire, Quebec. Amer. Mineral. 56.

Chao, G.Y. 1978. Monteregionite, a new hydrous sodium potassium yttrium silicate mineral from Mont St-Hilaire, Quebec. Can. Mineral. 16.

Chao, G.Y. 1980. Paranatrolite, a new zeolite from Mont St-Hilaire, Quebec. Can. Mineral. 18.

Chao, G.Y., Watkinson, D.H. & Chen, T.T. 1974a. Hilairite, $Na_2ZrSi_3O_9$ $3H_2O$, a new mineral from Mont St-Hilaire, Quebec. Can. Mineral. 12.

Chao, G.Y., Watkinson, D.H. 1974b Gaidonnayite, $Na_2ZrSi_3O_9$ $2H_2O$. a new mineral from Mont St-Hilaire, Quebec. Can. Mineral. 12.

Chao, G.Y., Mainwaring, P.R. & Baker, J. 1978. Donnayite, $NaCaSr_3(CO_3)$ $3H_2O$, a new mineral from Mont St-Hilaire, Quebec. Can. Mineral. 16.

Chao, G.Y., Chen, T.T. & Baker, J. 1980: Petarasite, a new hydrated sodium zirconium hydroxychlorosilicate mineral from Mont St-Hilaire, Quebec. Can. Mineral. 18.

Chao, G.Y. Baker, J., Sabina, A.P. & Roberts, A.C. 1985. Doyleite, a new polymorph of $Al(OH)_3$, and its relationship to bayerite, gibbsite and nordstrandite. Can. Mineral. 23.

Chen, T.T. & Chao, G.Y. 1980. Tetranatrolite from Mont St-Hilaire, Quebec. Can. Mineral. 18.

Coleman, L.C. & Robertson, B.T. 1981. Nahpoite Na_2HPO^4, a new mineral from the Big Fish River area, Yukon Territory. Can. Mineral. 19.

Elliot, D.G. 1982. Amethyst from the Thunder Bay region, Ontario. Mineral. Rec. 13.

Emslie, R.F., Morse, S.A. & Wheeler, E.P. 1972 (2nd ed.). Igneous rocks of central Labrador with emphasis on anorthosotic and related intrusions. Int. Geol. Cong., field excursion guidebook A54.

Ercit, T.S., Cerny, P. & Hawthorne, F.C. 1984. Wodginite crystal chemistry. Geol. Soc. Amer., Prog. with Abstracts 16.

Gait, R.I. & Harris, D.C. 1980. Arsenohauchecornite and tellurohauchecornite: new minerals in the hauchecornite group. Mineral. Mag. 43.

Grice, J.D. & Williams, R. 1979. The Jeffrey mine, Asbestos, Quebec. Mineral. Rec. 10.

Grice, J.D. & Gasparrini, E. 1981. Spertiniite, $Cu(OH)_2$, a new mineral from the Jeffrey mine, Quebec. Can. Mineral. 19.

Grice, J.D. & Gault, R.A. 1983. Lapis lazuli from Lake Harbour, Baffin Island, Canada. Rocks and Minerals 58.

Grice, J.D. & Robinson, G.W. 1984. Jeffreyite, $(Ca,Na)_2(Be,Al)Si_2(O,OH)_7$, a new mineral species and its relation to the melilite group. Can. Mineral. 22.

Grice, J.D., Ercit, T.S., Van Velthuizen, J. & Dunn, P.J. [1987]. Poudretteite, $KNa_2B_3Si_{12}O_{30}$, a new member of the osumilite group from Mont St-Hilaire, Quebec, and its crystal structure. Can. Mineral. 25. In press.

Hawley, J.E. & Stanton, R.L. 1962. The facts: the ores, their minerals, metals and distribution in the Sudbury ores: their mineralogy and origin. Can. Mineral. 7.

Holter, M.E. 1969. The middle devonian prairie evaporite of Saskatchewan. Saskatchewan Dept of Mineral Resources, Geol. Sciences Branch, Industrial Minerals Div., Rep. No. 123.

Jambor, J.L. 1971. Gangue mineralogy; in the silver-arsenide deposits of the Cobalt-Gowganda region. Ontario. Can. Mineral. 11.

Jambor, J.L., Fong, D.G. & Sabina, A.P. 1969. Dresserite, the new barium analogue of dundasite. Can. Mineral. 10.

Jambor, J.L., Sabina, A.P. & Sturman, B.D. 1977a. Hydrodresserite, a new Ba-Al carbonate from a silicocarbonatite sill, Montreal Island, Quebec. Can. Mineral. 15.

Jambor, J.L., Sabina, A.P., Roberts, A.C. & Sturman, B.D. 1977b. Strontiodresserite, a new Sr-Al carbonate from Montreal Island, Quebec. Can. Mineral. 15.

Jambor, J.L., Sturman, B.D. & Weatherly, G.C. 1980. Sabinaite, a new anhydrous zirconium-bearing carbonate mineral from Montreal Island, Quebec. Can. Mineral. 18.

Jambor, J.L., Sabina, A.P., Roberts, A.C. et al. 1984. Franconite, a new hydrated Na-Nb oxide mineral from Montreal Island, Quebec. Can. Mineral. 22.

Jambor, J.L., Sabina, A.P., Roberts, A.C. et al. 1986. Hochelagaite, a new calcium niobium oxide mineral from Montreal, Quebec. Can. Mineral. 24.

Kile, D.E. 1984. Amethyst deposits of the Thunder Bay area, Ontario, Canada. Rocks and Minerals 59.

Kissin, S.A., Owens, D.R. & Roberts, W.L. 1978. Cernyite, a copper-cadmium-tin sulfide with the stannite structure. Can. Mineral. 16.

London, D., Zolensky, M.E. & Roedder, E. 1987. Diomignite: natural $Li_2B_4O_7$ from the Tanco pegmatite, Bernic Lake, Manitoba. Can. Mineral. 25.

Mandarino, J.A. & Sturman, B.D. 1976. Kulanite, a new barium iron aluminum phosphate from the Yukon Territory, Canada. Can. Mineral. 14.

Mandarino, J.A., Sturman, B.D. & Corlett, M.I. 1977. Penikisite, the magnesium analogue of kulanite, from Yukon Territory. Can. Mineral. 15.

Mandarino, J.A., Sturman, B.D. & Corlett, M.I. 1978. Satterlyite, a new hydroxyl-bearing ferrous phosphate from the Big Fish River area, Yukon Territory. Can. Mineral. 16.

Mandarino, J.A., Chao, G.Y., Gault, R.A. & Herd, R.K. [1986]. Mineralogy and petrology of Mont St-Hilaire, Quebec. GAC, MAC, CBU joint annual meeting, field excursion guidebook 9A. In press.

Marble, L. & Regis, A. 1979. The minerals of Mont St-Hilaire. Rocks and Minerals 54.

Nagel, J. 1981. The Rock Candy mine, British Columbia. Mineral. Rec. 12.

Naldrett, A.J. 1984. Mineralogy and composition of the Sudbury ores in the geology and ore deposits of the Sudbury structure. Ont. Geol. Surv, Special Vol. 1.

Nickel, E.H., Rowland, J.F. & McAdam, R.C. 1963. Wodginite, a new tin-manganese tantalate from Wodgina, Australia and Bernic Lake, Manitoba. Can. Mineral. 7.

Perrault, G., Semenov, E.I., Bikova, A.V. & Capitonova, T.A. 1969. La lemoynite, un nouveau silicate hydrate de zirconium et de sodium de St-Hilaire, Quebec. Can. Mineral. 9.

Perrault, G., Harvey, Y. & Pertsowsky, R. 1975. La yofortierite, un nouveau silicate hydrate de manganese de St-Hilaire, Quebec. Can. Mineral. 13.

Perrault, G. & Szymanski, J.T. 1982. Steacyite, a new name, and a re-evaluation of the nomenclature of "ekanite"-group minerals. Can. Mineral. 20.

Petruk, W. 1971. Mineralogical characteristics of the deposits and textures of the ore minerals; in the silver-arsenide deposits of the Cobalt-Gowganda region, Ontario. Can. Mineral. 11.

Petruk, W. 1972. Larosite, a new copper-lead-bismuth sulphide. Can. Mineral. 11.

Petruk, W., Harris, D.C. & Stewart, J.M. 1969. Langisite, a new mineral, and the rare minerals cobalt pentlandite, siegenite, parkerite and bravoite from the Langis mine, Cobalt-Gowganda area, Ontario. Can. Mineral. 9.

Petruk, W., Harris, D.C. & Stewart, J.M. 1971a. Characteristics of the arsenides, sulpharsenides and antimonides; in the silver-arsenide deposits of the Cobalt-Gowganda region, Ontario. Can. Mineral. 11.

Petruk, W., Harris, D.C., Cabri, L.J. & Stewart, J.M. 1971b. Characteristics of the silver-antimony minerals; in the silver-arsenide deposits of the Cobalt-Gowganda region, Ontario. Can. Mineral. 11.

Petruk, W. & staff. 1971c. Characteristics of the sulphides; in the silver-arsenide deposits of the Cobalt-Gowganda region, Ontario. Can. Mineral. 11.

Ramik, R.A., Sturman, B.C., Dunn, P.J. & Povarennykh, A.S. 1980. Tancoite, a new lithium sodium aluminum phosphate from the Tanco pegmatite, Bernic Lake, Manitoba. Can. Mineral. 18.

Ramik, R.A., Sturman, B.D., Roberts, A.C., & Dunn, P.J. 1983. Viitaniemiite from the Francon quarry, Montreal, Quebec. Can. Mineral. 21.

Roberts, A.C., Ansell, H.G., Grice, J.D. & Ramik, R.A. 1985. Rapidcreekite, a new hydrated calcium sulfate-carbonate from the Rapid Creek area, Yukon Territory. Can. Mineral. 23.

Roberts, A.C., Sabina, A.P. Bonardi, M. et al. 1986. Montroyalite, a new hydrated Sr-Al hydroxycarbonate from the Francon Quarry, Montreal, Quebec. Can. Mineral. 24.

Robertson, B.T. 1982. Occurrence of epigenetic phosphate minerals in a phosphatic iron-formation, Yukon. Can. Mineral. 20.

Sabina, A.P. 1964. Rocks and minerals for the collector: Bay of Fundy area; New Brunswick-Nova Scotia. GSC pap. 64-10.

Sabina, A.P. 1972. Rocks and minerals for the collector: the Alaska Highway; Dawson Creek, British Columbia to Yukon/Alaska border. GSC pap. 72-32.

Sabina, A.P. 1974. Rocks and minerals for the collector: Cobalt-Belleterre-Timmins; Ontario and Quebec. GSC pap. 73-13.

Sabina, A.P. 1979. Minerals of the Francon quarry (Montreal Island): a progress report. GSC pap. 79-1A.

Sabina, A.P. 1986. Rocks and minerals for the collector: Bancroft-Parry Sound. Southern Ontario. GSC misc. rep. 39.

Sabina, A.P., Jambor, J.L. & Plant, A.G. 1968. Weloganite, a new strontium zirconium carbonate from Montreal Island, Canada. Can. Mineral. 9.

Skinner, B.J., Jambor, J.L. & Ross, M. 1966. McKinstryite, a new copper-silver sulfide. Econ. Geol. 61.

Sturman, B.D. & Mandarino, J.A. 1976. Baricite, the magnesium analogue of vivianite from Yukon Territory, Canada. Can. Mineral. 14.

Sturman, B.D., Mandarino, J.A. 7 Corlett, M.I. 1977. Maricite, a sodium iron phosphate, from the Big Fish River area, Yukon Territory, Canada. Can. Mineral. 15.

Sturman, B.D., Peacor, D.R. & Dunn, P.J. 1981a. Wicksite, a new mineral from northeastern Yukon Territory. Can. Mineral. 19.

Sturman, B.D., Mandarino, J.A., Mrose, M.E. & Dunn, P.J. 1981b. Gormanite, $Fe^{2+}_3Al_4(PO_4)_4(OH)_6$ $2H_2O$, the ferrous analogue of souzalite, and new date for souzalite. Can. Mineral. 19.

Sturman, B.D. & Dunn, P.J. 1984. Garyansellite, a new mineral from Yukon Territory, Canada. Amer. Mineral. 69.

Wight, Q. & Chao, G.Y. 1986. Mont St-Hilaire revisited. Rocks and Minerals, 61.